Editor-in-Chief and Founder:
   Lyndon H. LaRouche, Jr.
Editorial Board: *Lyndon H. LaRouche, Jr. , Helga
   Zepp-LaRouche, Robert Ingraham, Tony
   Papert, Gerald Rose, Dennis Small, Jeffrey
   Steinberg, William Wertz*
Co-Editors: *Robert Ingraham, Tony Papert*
Managing Editor: *Nancy Spannaus*
Technology: *Marsha Freeman*
Books: *Katherine Notley*
Ebooks: *Richard Burden*
Graphics: *Alan Yue*
Photos: *Stuart Lewis*
Circulation Manager: *Stanley Ezrol*

INTELLIGENCE DIRECTORS
Counterintelligence: *Jeffrey Steinberg, Michele
   Steinberg*
Economics: *John Hoefle, Marcia Merry Baker,
   Paul Gallagher*
History: *Anton Chaitkin*
Ibero-America: *Dennis Small*
Russia and Eastern Europe: *Rachel Douglas*
United States: *Debra Freeman*

INTERNATIONAL BUREAUS
Bogotá: *Miriam Redondo*
Berlin: *Rainer Apel*
Copenhagen: *Tom Gillesberg*
Houston: *Harley Schlanger*
Lima: *Sara Madueño*
Melbourne: *Robert Barwick*
Mexico City: *Gerardo Castilleja Chávez*
New Delhi: *Ramtanu Maitra*
Paris: *Christine Bierre*
Stockholm: *Ulf Sandmark*
United Nations, N.Y.C.: *Leni Rubinstein*
Washington, D.C.: *William Jones*
Wiesbaden: *Göran Haglund*

ON THE WEB
e-mail: eirns@larouchepub.com
www.larouchepub.com
www.executiveintelligencereview.com
www.larouchepub.com/eiw
Webmaster: *John Sigerson*
Assistant Webmaster: *George Hollis*
Editor, Arabic-language edition: *Hussein Askary*

EIR (ISSN 0273-6314) *is published weekly
(50 issues), by EIR News Service, Inc.,
P.O. Box 17390, Washington, D.C. 20041-0390.
(703) 297-8434*

European Headquarters: E.I.R. GmbH, Postfach
Bahnstrasse 9a, D-65205, Wiesbaden, Germany
Tel: 49-611-73650
Homepage: http://www.eir.de
e-mail: info@eir.de
Director: Georg Neudecker

Montreal, Canada: 514-461-1557
eir@eircanada.ca

Denmark: EIR - Danmark, Sankt Knuds Vej 11,
basement left, DK-1903 Frederiksberg, Denmark.
Tel.: +45 35 43 60 40, Fax: +45 35 43 87 57. e-mail:
eirdk@hotmail.com.

Mexico City: EIR, Sor Juana Inés de la Cruz 242-2
Col. Agricultura C.P. 11360
Delegación M. Hidalgo, México D.F.
Tel. (5525) 5318-2301
eirmexico@gmail.com

Canada Post Publication Sales Agreement
#40683579

Postmaster: Send all address changes to *EIR*, P.O.
Box 17390, Washington, D.C. 20041-0390.

Signed articles in *EIR* represent the views of the authors,
and not necessarily those of the Editorial Board.

How To Rescue Our Forgotten Men and Women with President Trump

Are They All Simply Crazy —Or What?

by Michael G. Steger

July 16—Under the cover of exposing Russian collusion with the Trump team, the entire political establishment in the United States is committing total self-destruction. Why? Why choose to go down in flames with a transparent lie—Russian meddling in the election—when everyone now knows that it was the DNC which meddled against Bernie Sanders? And meddled on behalf of Hillary and against Trump, along with CNN, in coordination with a British-Atlantic spy matrix that includes MI-6, Fusion GPS, and CrowdStrike—along with operatives such as Christopher Steele, John Brennan, and James Comey?

EDITORIAL

It was one thing to lie in the hope that somehow Trump might be prevented from taking the oath of office—as unlikely a prospect as that always was. It's one thing to keep the story alive as the rationale for an independent counsel—as corrupt as that might be in the face of the truth. But to ceaselessly focus on stories of greater and greater irrelevance, while hyperventilating each time with greater hysteria? Accusations of "treason" for simply holding a twenty-minute meeting? The enemies of our nation, without and within, may be incredibly evil—even to the point of launching a nuclear war—but they are not *entirely* stupid.

CNN has dragged its ratings down below those of "Nick at Night" on cable television. The *New York Times* is shrinking into nothingness before our eyes; the only thing growing is its reputation for war-mongering and lies. What is the *Washington Post* now, but a public utility for leaking intelligence agents, with a slogan which is fitting only for a Greek tragedy's self-fulfilling prophecy—"Democracy Dies in Darkness." Along with NBC, and the other main networks, they are all committing a sort of suicide, repeating lie after lie, night after night—all while the American people suffer under the policies which the networks have endorsed for the last 20, if not the last 50 years.

If you need proof, just look at the election results.

Those policies included the deindustrialization program of the 1970s—Wall Street's greenie, pro-drug, anti-technology policy. Remember 18% interest rates? There is no faster way to end investment into critical long-term national infrastructure than Volcker's late 1970s program. It was in the late 1970s when our nation's aging infrastructure required a new platform of low-interest credit. Instead, we got the Savings and Loan scandal and the takedown of U.S. industry.

However, it was the last twenty years that saw the blatant neglect of our nation's industry and population—in other words, a total disregard for the nation's long-term survival—turned into a policy of psychotic terror. Beginning with the phony impeachment coup run against Bill Clinton—who in 1998 threatened to change the global financial system back towards an industrial orientation as Lyndon LaRouche advised him—the terror has only increased. In the face of financial blowout, in Asia in 1997, the breakdown of Long-Term Capital Management (LTCM) and the nascent hedge fund industry in 1998, and then again with the dot-com bubble in 2000, the financial system was in systemic breakdown. Then comes George W. Bush, with zero political power or mandate. That is, no political control over a population as the economic system blows out underneath their feet. And not just long-term survival, but their short term survival has now become threatened.

Thus comes 9-11—a British-Saudi provocation intended to allow installation of a dictatorship—just as Lyndon LaRouche had warned in January, 2001, that some such provocation would ensue. Dick Cheney couldn't quite achieve the dictatorship he wanted, but he came near to dictatorial control over the population. Cultural hysteria was invoked, not unlike the 1960s, but this time for war. Police-state measures were introduced. A program of perpetual war was launched against all nations that could oppose a global financial dictatorship—including targeting the nuclear powers, Russia and China.

To try to preserve the rotting financial system, a massive housing bubble was fuelled, bringing the crumbs of blue-collar construction jobs and white-collar paper-pushing jobs with it. But this just pumped up the Wall Street bubble all the faster, and in 2007 it cracked. The system is again about to burst—a system of debt and corruption on Wall Street, already ten times bigger than in 2000. By September of 2008, the system is in total disintegration; Cheney is threatening martial law. The $20 trillion plus bailout begins—all under the eye of British agent Barack Obama.

Obama, unbeknownst to most of his supporters, was chosen to be the next President by this fascist coup, specifically because he would continue the Bush legacy—the fascist police state, the perpetual war regime, and the non-stop bailout of Wall Street's crime system.

Hillary Clinton submitted to this fascist coup. She would have continued it were she elected in 2016, and the American people knew it. Had she been elected, we would likely already be engaged in a potentially nuclear World War III.

However, she was not!!

Donald Trump, who first ran against the Bush legacy in the Republican Party, and then against the Obama faction in the Democratic party, was, in fact, running a

Creative Commmons

Wall Street

Presidential campaign against the fascist coup first launched against Bill Clinton and brought to full power through the British/Saudi orchestrated 9-11 attack.

The Financial System Is Ready to Blow

So—what does this have to do with the massive Russian collusion story the mainstream media can't stop talking about—even while a majority of even the Democratic Party voters don't buy it?

The Wall Street system of massive debt, fraud, and crime, is now ten times bigger than in 2008—and that's a hundred times larger than in 2000!

That system is going to blow sky-high, and their police-state control system is no longer there! No Bush, no Obama, no Hillary! The entire system is going to blow, possibly as early as the end of this summer, while others put the late date at early next year.

At that point, none of these institutions—the political parties, the financial institutions like JP Morgan-Chase or Wells Fargo, the mainstream media companies, the colleges, or the entire culture for that matter—will have any legitimacy. The system is at the utter fag end, and there is only one way out.

A new principle must be introduced, premised on the fundamental distinction of mankind as above and superior to all merely animal species. This principle, and its policy program, is most succinctly expressed in Lyndon LaRouche's June 10, 2014 *Four Laws*.

The credit principle established in that document, provides for the long-term requirements of mankind's development, while also addressing the immediate short-term requirements for the continuity of our society. Nothing less will suffice. We are at revolutionary breakdown of the system, and the only solution is the adoption of a higher principle of mode of operations, in accord with the creative and immortal legacy of mankind.

'Put This Organization Into a Campaign Mode, Like You've Never Seen It Before!'

July 16—Let us be very clear, crystal clear, as to what constitutes the nature of the current strategic situation—and what that means for all of us.

Helga Zepp-LaRouche led a discussion with organizers from throughout the United States today. In that discussion she posed a challenge—an urgent call—to dramatically escalate the battle in which we are now engaged. She described our current situation as a "dual power" environment, one in which great accomplishments have been achieved over the recent months, but great dangers still exist. She warned that we are now facing the likelihood of a near-term financial collapse far worse than that of 2008, citing this as the "Sword of Damocles" that is threatening the entire world, a collapse which could destroy all of the positive achievements of the recent period. As she put it, by the end of the Summer, we could be in "the biggest crisis ever."

Victory in this fight is absolutely possible. But, as Mrs. LaRouche stressed, we are not yet fully mobilized to achieve that victory. Passivity, doubts, and fears have crept into the hearts of many. This applies to full-time organizers, part-time organizers, volunteers, subscribers, contributors, and new friends and recruits who are joining this movement. We need to build this organization into an irresistible force which will stop at nothing short of victory. All doubts, all hesitations, all passivity must be swept away, and a guidon must be raised to expand this movement quantitatively and qualitatively outward, through recruitment and a rapidly expanding political mobilization.

What Has Been Accomplished to Date

Many, many good things have happened since the inauguration of Donald Trump as U.S. President. Of paramount importance has been the dramatic change in U.S. relations with Russia and China. Beginning with President Trump's April meeting with Chinese President Xi Jinping at Mar-a-Lago, Florida, then continuing through subsequent meetings and discussions between the two Presidents, and including the sending of a high level American delegation to the Beijing Belt and Road Forum in May, a stunning breakthrough has been accomplished in U.S.-China relations. At the same time, the meeting which took place on July 7 between President Trump and Russian President Putin at the G-20 Summit in Hamburg, Germany, holds out the same promise for improved relations. After the meeting, the Russian President stated that Trump was far different from the caricature portrayed in the news media. Putin pointed out that, during their discussion, Trump listened, that he was frank, and that this represented real promise for an improvement in relations between the two nations.

What Trump supporters, and others, within the United States must be brought to understand, is that these breakthroughs in U.S. relations with Russia and China are not only the greatest accomplishment of his Presidency to date—but that they are in fact historic, and are pregnant with potential for much greater changes to come. Since Sept. 11, 2001, the United States has opted for a state of permanent war: Sixteen years of warfare, the longest in the nation's history. Worse, since the Presidencies of Bush and Obama, the trajectory has been one of a rapidly escalating military confrontation with both Russia and China toward strategic war, world war. President Trump has now taken the first decisive actions to change course. This is real, not hype, and as Mrs. LaRouche put it, "This is excellent"!

All of the efforts to impeach or otherwise bring down

President Trump have nothing whatsoever to do with alleged Russian "hacking" of the election, nor even with Trump's domestic policies. This is the Bush/Obama War Party gnashing their teeth and flailing out, as their designs to subdue the world by threats and force begin to vanish in the breeze of a new paradigm. Britain's Theresa May and Germany's Angela Merkel may still both be locked into the old geopolitical mindset, but without the United States, their strategic intentions are a non-starter, and both London and Wall Street know that.

The Achilles' Heel

The financial policy of inflationary "quantitative easing" has reached its end-point. The U.S. debt bubble is now greater than in 2008, with corporate and government debt leading the way. The utter failure of Dodd-Frank and other half-baked measures to control this crisis, is now apparent to all. Combined with this monetary/financial crisis, there is an escalating breakdown of the physical economy, and increased impoverishment of the population. This is across the board: agriculture, manufacturing, transportation, power generation, and most visibly, the utter breakdown of basic U.S. infrastructure, as typified by the "Summer of Hell" transit crisis now under way in New York City.

We are facing the inevitability of both a financial blow-out worse than 2008, one which could break out at any moment, as well as a deepening social crisis in which the frustration, rage, and desperation of the American people could find means of expression that become very dangerous.

During his campaign, and in numerous statements since his election, President Donald Trump has forcefully voiced his intention to rebuild American industrial and economic might. He has spoken of a trillion dollars in infrastructure investment; he has called for the immediate reinstatement of Franklin Roosevelt's Glass Steagall banking legislation; he became the first President in more than a century to speak of the American System of Economy; and he has repeatedly praised the economic outlook of Alexander Hamilton and Abraham Lincoln.

The problem—and it is a very serious problem—is that seven months into his administration, he has yet to move forcefully to carry through on any of this. The unprecedented massive attacks on Trump are at least partially aimed to sabotage such bold initiatives, and certainly the presence of Steven Mnuchin and other Wall Street partisans within his administration has not helped.

What must be understood is that the economic policy enunciated in Lyndon LaRouche's "Four Laws," a policy which is fully coherent in its intent with Donald Trump's stated intentions, must be carried out now. Such action can not wait until "after the crash," amidst conditions of crisis, collapse, and chaos. The positive accomplishments—and the promise of even greater accomplishments—which President Trump has made through his foreign policy initiatives, will all be swept aside, like water cascading through a broken dam, in the wake of a banking/financial blowout. War will be back on the agenda.

What This Means to You

We need to build the power, the resources and the manpower of this movement. Not because it is "our" movement," but because it represents the one critical factor which could make the difference between victory and defeat. Our future and the future of everyone you know depends on the outcome of this battle. The fight is engaged right now. Everyone can contribute to the effort.

In one sense, the fight now for LaRouche's "Four Laws" is the culmination of a battle which Lyndon LaRouche launched more than forty years ago. LaRouche's record speaks for itself. He was right in 1971. He was right in 1988. And he was right in 2008. Lyndon LaRouche is the greatest economist in the world today. The Hamiltonian banking and economic measures which LaRouche specifies in his "Four Laws" will work to solve this crisis; nothing else will get the job done. Every week we reprint strategic articles by LaRouche in the *Executive Intelligence Review*, so as to provide the necessary means whereby readers of *EIR* might master the principles necessary to successfully engage in this battle.

Don't think small. Grow your mind. This is not a domestic policy fight within the United States. The issue is War or Peace, a future or no future, economic collapse or an unprecedented explosion of economic development. A victory in securing the passage of Glass-Steagall and the adoption of national banking and credit policies, together with the type of science-driver approach which the United States used to be famous for, is the means by which the War Party can be stopped, the U.S. and world economy rebuilt, and a better future created. But everyone *must* do his or her part! No one can afford to be a spectator.

EIR Contents

www.larouchepub.com Volume 44, Number 29, July 21, 2017

Cover This Week

The Good Samaritan by John Quincy Adams Ward (1867), in the Boston Public Gardens.

wikipedia

REPORT

The Promise of Fusion Rocketry

by Joel DeJean

This is a transcription of the oral report given by Joel DeJean to a LaRouche PAC class in Houston on June 24. He was introduced by Kesha Rogers of the LaRouche PAC Policy Committee, who noted that the subject is not simply the technology of fusion power, but the development of fusion power as a way to ignite the advance of mankind. Extraordinary developments are taking place, she said, and DeJean's report has implications beyond

science as such. Right now we need to make a total scientific breakthrough for mankind. There are new developments in research that will take the American-Chinese cooperation for the New Silk Road to the next leap. That is what fusion power and cooperation in space will do, because we're not just talking about the Chinese coming here to help us build our railways systems and rebuild some dams and ports, and then going home.

FIGURE 1

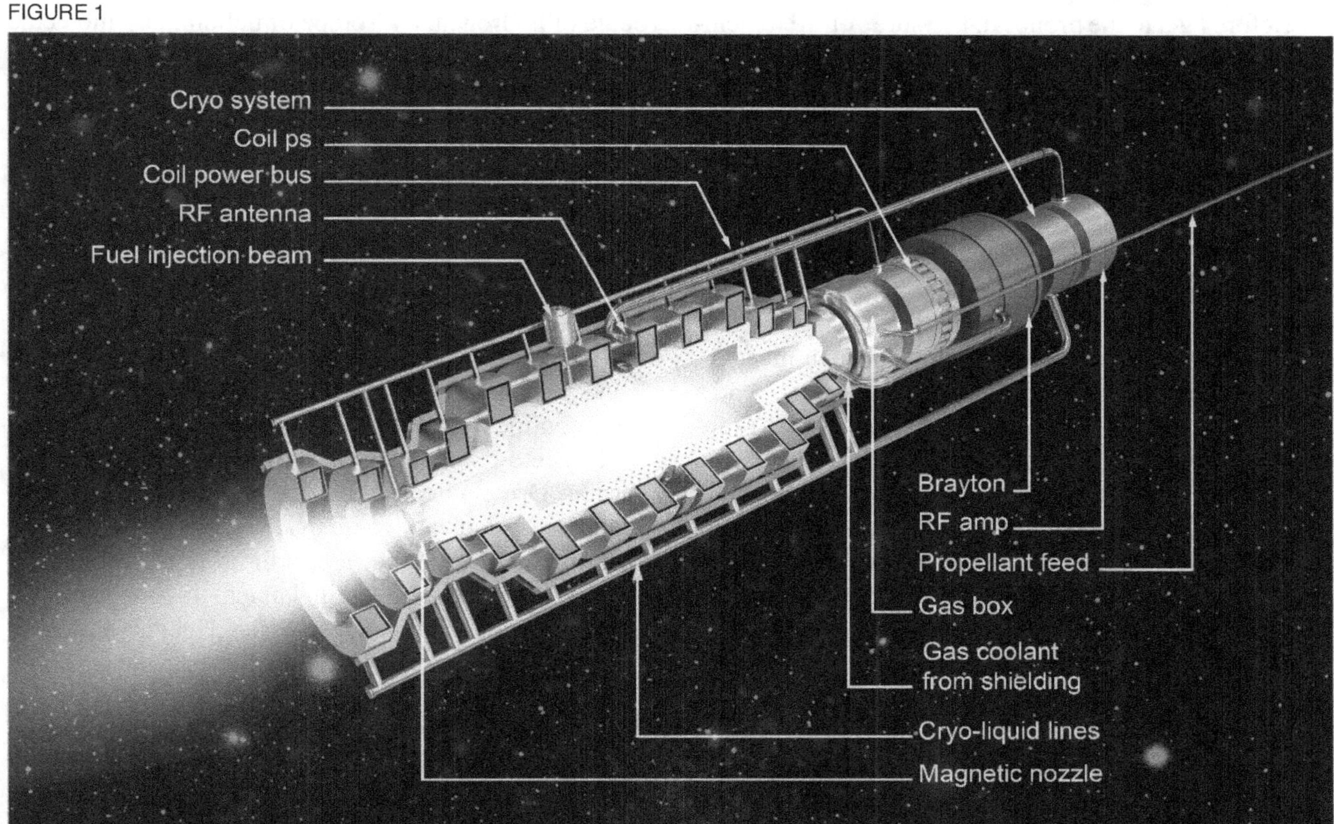

Artist's rendering of a Direct Fusion Drive engine with interior cutout to show detail of the magnetic coils.

Rather, we must ask, "What is the next mission of cooperation for mankind?" And the answer, she said, is space cooperation, and space cooperation driven by the development of fusion power as the key source for increasing the energy available to mankind.

A few weeks ago we had a conference call on the Space Silk Road, and discussed some of the latest developments on how to get to low Earth orbit. Additionally, Brian Lantz discussed some of the developments around nuclear thermal rockets—fission-based rockets that will be useful to go between low Earth orbit and the Moon. Then Kesha sent me the link to an article about a recent design for a fusion rocket to go to Mars, a rocket with an engine about the size of a refrigerator, and Megan Beets found another article about it. I called Michael Paluzsek, the president of Princeton Satellite Systems, which developed this proposal a few years ago, and he sent me the proposal itself. His team proposes a manned mission to Mars, using what it calls a Direct Fusion Drive rocket engine. It could accomplish a round trip in something like 310 days.

Before I get to the proposal, I'm sure you all remember that *Curiosity*, which is still functioning on Mars, left Earth orbit on Nov. 26, 2011, using a chemical rocket, and landed on Mars on Aug. 6, 2012. So it took more than eight months to get from Earth to Mars— eight months! During its voyage, the team got readings from sensors measuring the amount of cosmic radiation that would hit a traveller en route to Mars for nine months. It turned out that it would be something like the equivalent one CT scan a week for a whole year. Combine that with the low-gravity atrophy of your muscles, living at microgravity for months. If you were to send a crew to Mars using chemical rockets, you would probably end up with a dead crew, before they even got to Mars orbit. At the least, by the time they got to Mars orbit they certainly wouldn't be very functional.

What piqued my interest in the design of the Direct Fusion Drive, was not only that it was using compact magnetic confinement, but that it was also using the combination of deuterium and helium-3 as its fuel.

Why fusion? Why not use more efficient chemical rockets? Or why not use nuclear thermal rockets, in which a fission core heats a gas, and that gas is used as the propellant? Well, the most efficient chemical propellant rocket that we have, uses the reaction of hydrogen gas with oxygen, $H_2 + O_2$, to get H_2O, or water.

This reaction releases 8 electron volts of energy. Now fusion is what happens in the Sun—and we've already achieved fusion on Earth, called the H-bomb; what we are seeking is controlled fusion, so that you can control the release of the energy. In this case, we use an isotope of hydrogen called deuterium, which has one proton and one neutron, instead of having just one proton. With it, we use an isotope of helium, called helium-3. Normal helium is helium-4, which has two protons and two neutrons, but helium-3 has two protons and only one neutron. We want to fuse those two atoms.

To fuse them, we need high temperatures, and we need a certain density of what is called the plasma— and we'll go through that—and we need enough time under these conditions so that you can have these elements fuse, creating a new element—helium-4 plus a proton. The energy released from this fusion reaction, called the D-He3 or deuterium-helium-3 reaction, is 18 *million* electron volts. So in the chemical and fusion reactions, you have only the elements of hydrogen, helium, and oxygen—an isotope of hydrogen, or a molecule of hydrogen, an isotope of helium, or a molecule of oxygen—but the fusion process releases more than a million times more energy in electron volts, a million times more energy than any chemical reaction, whether it's combustion, the process inside an electric battery, or whatever.

Now I want to go through the concept of this rocket design. The Direct Fusion Drive engine is based on developments at Princeton University. The Princeton Plasma Physics Laboratory (PPPL) has been working on fusion for decades, even though it has had major setbacks in funding. PPPL is using the concept of magnetic confinement of the plasma to get fusion.

Princeton Satellite Systems' idea is to use its Direct Fusion Drive engine together with NASA's Space Launch System, and with NASA's Orion spacecraft carrying the crew as far as Earth orbit. (Orion is now being developed.) You will launch this ensemble to Earth orbit to reach the Deep Space Habitat, a module now being developed by NASA for living and working, which will travel between Earth orbit and Mars orbit. The motor in this concept is six of the Direct Fusion Drive rocket engines. You launch the Deep Space Habitat into Earth orbit with the Space Launch System, which has about the lift capacity of the old Saturn V. The Saturn V rocket from the Apollo Program days

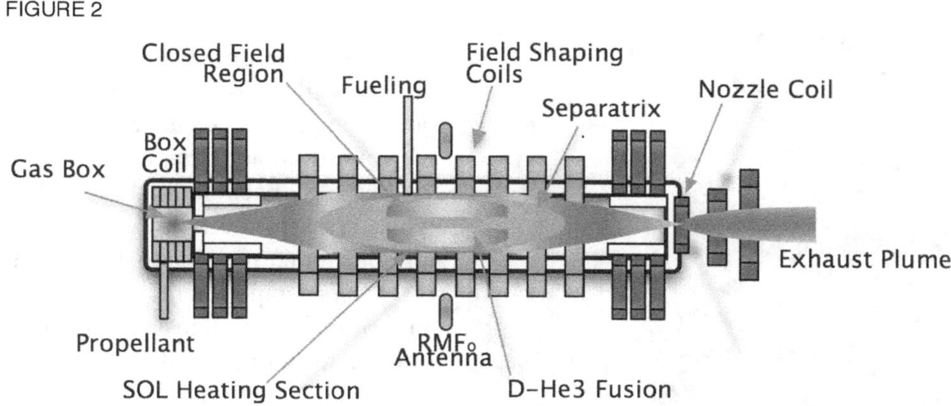

Schematic of Direct Fusion Drive core. Deuterium gas, introduced into the gas box, is ionized there. This newly formed plasma flows to the right in the scrape-off layer (SOL), where the electrons are heated as they pass over the field-reversed configuration region.

could lift 100 metric tons of payload into low Earth orbit, if you remember, which included the capsule, the landers, all the equipment, and the crew.

So what you do now is, first, launch that Deep Space Habitat with the fusion motor into Earth orbit. Then, after everything has tested out in orbit, you launch the crew into the same Earth orbit in the Orion capsule, for transfer to the Deep Space Habitat. Finally, the Direct Fusion Drive engines power the Deep Space Habitat to leave Earth orbit and head to Mars (see **Figure 1**).

To get to low Earth orbit, you have to reach a speed of 17,500 mph. So if you use your app and locate the space station—you can actually see it going over at night—it's travelling at 17,500 mph to stay in orbit. Now, to leave Earth orbit you have to reach a speed of 25,000 mph, so that you can escape Earth's gravity—to go to the Moon, Mars, or Pluto. What's fascinating about the Direct Fusion Drive, shown in **Figure 2**—you see the exhaust on the right—is that it uses the Princeton Field-Reversed Configuration to confine the plasma.

Let's review what a plasma is. If we start with a gas, like the air in this room, at high enough temperatures, the electrons orbiting hydrogen or oxygen or any atom, will be stripped away, so we will have ions and electrons separated from each other—and that's called a high-temperature plasma.

The Direct Fusion Drive system uses deuterium, which is a heavy isotope of hydrogen (having an extra neutron), tanks of liquid deuterium, and liquid helium-

3, which is injected into the plasma chamber.

You may have seen the huge magnetic confinement systems that use a tokamak—a doughnut-shaped or torus-shaped vessel that has magnets going around its circumference (along the tube of the torus) and also at right angles (wrapping around the tube of the torus)—and when the magnets are in operation, they will confine the plasma, keeping it away from the inner walls of the torus.

Now to attain fusion, the plasma has to reach temperatures of close to 100 million degrees Centigrade. You can imagine if you had plasma at 100 million degrees hitting the side of a vessel, made of any metal, it would vaporize that metal. So you contain it with magnetic fields.

The Princeton Field-Reversed Configuration uses—instead of a torus—a cylinder, with high-temperature magnets. When the helium-3 and deuterium gases are injected into the chamber, they are heated to the point of ionization with radio waves in the megahertz range, creating a plasma. The plasma, because it has charged ions and electrons, will create an electric field. And electric fields always create magnetic fields. The field created here will be the reverse of the *applied* magnetic field, and this will provide the containment. That allows us to have the plasma contained within about a 2 meter diameter inside that cylinder. So the dimensions are 2 meters in diameter and 10 meters long.

Once you ionize the gas, then you heat it further, to high enough temperatures to achieve fusion. Now once you achieve fusion, because the reaction products, helium-4 and the proton, are positively charged, they can be manipulated using magnetic fields in what's called a magnetic nozzle. If you look at the Space Shuttle when it launches, you see the nozzle directing the propellant—you can see the swivelling of the nozzles. But if you were to use an ordinary nozzle with high-temperature plasmas, you would melt the nozzle. So you have magnetic fields in the nozzle so that you can direct the exhaust.

PFRC-2 device under assembly.

PFRC-2 device during operation.

In a chemical reaction, the exhaust velocity of the propellant is on the order of 10 kilometers per second, while in a fusion reaction you can get exhaust velocities of over 25,000 km per second or even higher, because of the high energy of a fusion reaction. You can adjust the exhaust velocity. You can get an increase in thrust through an increase in propellant velocity. This Direct Fusion Drive will not only produce the exhaust from the propellant, giving you the thrust to get to Mars, but it will also generate electric power, to power the entire spacecraft for your mission to Mars.

Let's go back to Figure 2. The white areas in the figure are shielding. In another reaction that is typical for fusion experiments, deuterium and tritium are used instead of deuterium and helium-3—tritium being another isotope of hydrogen that has one proton and two neutrons. Using deuterium and tritium produces almost as much energy as deuterium and helium-3. However, most of the energy is carried off by a neutral particle, the neutron, which cannot be controlled by magnetic fields because it has no charge. The neutrons will hit the sides of the engine and will even penetrate the crew compartment, so you have to provide enough shielding to protect the crew from these high-energy neutrons.

But some shielding is needed even for deuterium-helium-3 fusion. Even though this reaction produces only positive charges, deuterium-deuterium reactions will also occur. While 95% of the fusion products will be charged helium-4 or a proton, about 5% will be high-energy neutrons and some tritium, so that you still need to have some neutron-shielding while the fusion process is going on.

Figure 3 shows the Princeton Field-Reversed Configuration as embodied in the PFRC-2 device while it was being assembled. They have already built this. They haven't achieved full fusion power yet, but this work is being done under NASA contract through the NASA Innovative Advanced Concept Program, which is intended to fund projects that could pay off in 10 to 100 years in the future.

Figure 4 shows the PFRC-2 device during experimentall operation.

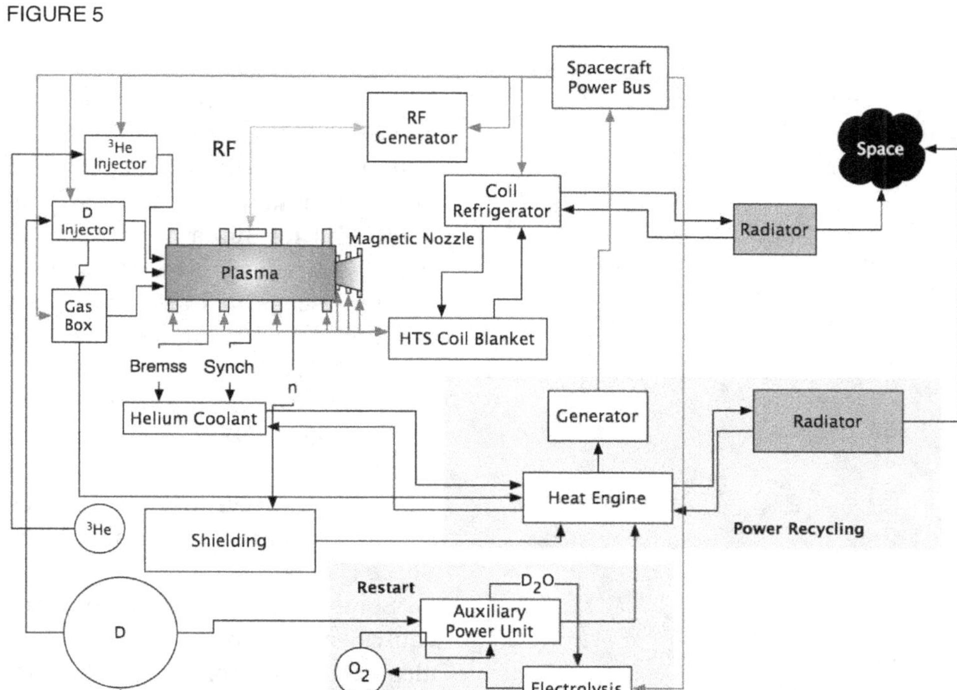

Direct Fusion Drive subsystems.

When I talked to Dr. Paluszek, he said that he and his team are ready for Phase 3, but they lack funding. Now, a measly 20 million bucks—we're talking about a few cruise missiles, we're talking about one-tenth of a F-35 fighter—would pay for the next phase. And they

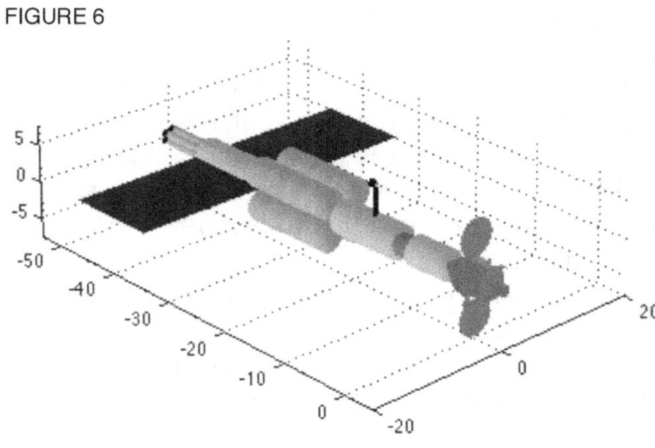

The Mars transfer vehicle with a docked Orion spacecraft on the far right. Next to the Orion are two high-gain dish antennas and then the Deep Space Habitat—two gray tubular units. The clustered, large brown tanks hold deuterium. The bundled Direct Fusion Drive engines are at the far end (shown in brown), beyond the heat dissipation panels.

project that once they prove that they can heat the plasma to high enough temperatures, and that it is dense enough, and that they can have long enough confinement time so that they can achieve fusion—then they can use these engines for a demonstration flight to Mars.

Figure 5 takes us beyond the plasma chamber. Here we see the subsystems necessary to make things happen in the chamber.

A lot of testing is required to prove the concept of the field-reversed configuration. The concept goes back to testing in the Los Alamos National Laboratory in the 1990s. It has also been tested in the Pacific Northwest National Laboratory in Redmond, Washington and the U.S. Naval Laboratory in San Diego. Some testing has also been done at the Air Force Research Laboratory in Dayton, Ohio. So there's a lot of research going on. Lockheed Martin is working on a compact magnetic fusion reactor that would be about the size of a truck. So, if they can divert some of that money from that F-35 program into fusion, we can get there a lot quicker. [laughter]

The Mars transfer vehicle, shown in **Figure 6**, consists of the the Direct Fusion Drive and Deep Space Habitat, where the crew of either four or six will live and work. The Deep Space Habitat, as you can see in **Figure 7**, is like a small space station. It has laboratory

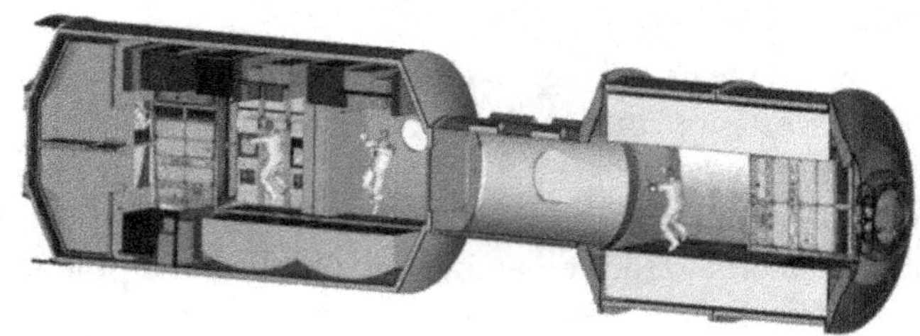

NASA's Deep Space Habitat.

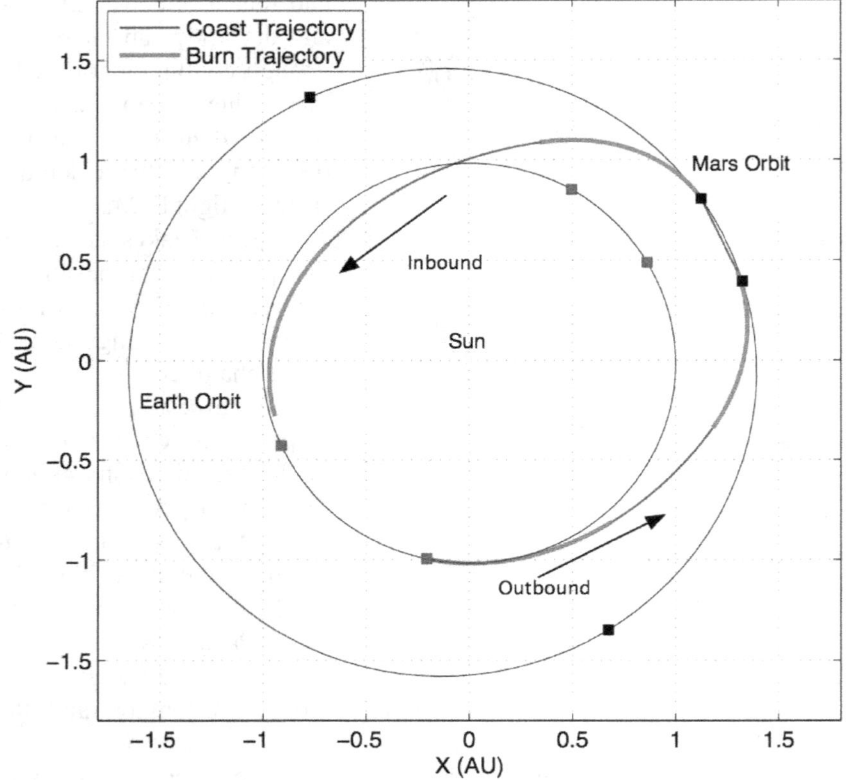

A round trip mission to Mars takes only 310 days, including 30 days in Mars orbit. The outer orbit is that of Mars.

and experimental compartments, as well as exercise rooms, so you can live in that habitat.

A round trip mission to Mars will take only 310 days, including 30 days in Mars orbit (see **Figure 8**). The Deep Space Habitat is driven by six Direct Fusion Drive rocket engines. Each engine produces 11.5 megawatts of power, so the whole assembly will produce about 70 megawatts, which is the power of the heavy nuclear-powered aircraft carriers such as the *USS Nimitz.*

When the crew is on board in Earth orbit, and everything tests out, the engines will burn to leave Earth orbit, followed by a coasting period, so the travel time would be about 140 days. That's still a little long, but this is the first step. Remember that the Wright brothers' first aircraft flew at about 40 mph. Now we go a little faster, but this is the first step.

The craft will achieve escape velocity and continue to burn and then coast for a while. When it approaches Mars, the crew will have to turn on the motors to brake. The idea is to orbit Mars, not to fly by. So it will brake, achieve an orbital insertion, and then stay in Mars orbit for 30 days. To return to Earth, they will again fire the motors, achieve escape velocity from Mars orbit, and coast a while. Once they approach Earth, they have to slow down and enter Earth's orbit. At that point, another Orion capsule will be sent to Earth orbit to bring the crew back, because you won't come back to Earth's surface with the Deep Space Habitat.

Something like this would be the equivalent of Apollo 8. If you remember December 1968—the first time man left Earth's orbit was in December 1968. And if you remember, when the crew in the Apollo 8 approached the Moon, it was not immediately known whether they were down. NASA had to make precise calculations. In the movie, *Hidden Figures*, you see them doing the calculations. Because you have a moving capsule, you have the speed in orbit—so everything had to be worked out to the *decimal point*. They went around the Moon, and of course you can't hear any radio signals once they're behind the Moon, and so there was a period of *minutes* when you didn't know whether they would make it, or they would go into the Sun, or what. And then they came back, and you heard them reciting from Genesis—it was Christmas Eve.

So this Mars orbital mission would be the equivalent breakthrough.

At the end of the paper, the authors mention that you could also use these Direct Fusion Drive rockets to deflect an asteroid coming at you. You could get to an asteroid and deflect it before it hits the Earth.

They also mention that Direct Fusion Drive could be used for robotic missions, such as a mission to Pluto. The recent Horizon mission to Pluto took nine years to get to Pluto, they say, but it didn't have enough fuel left

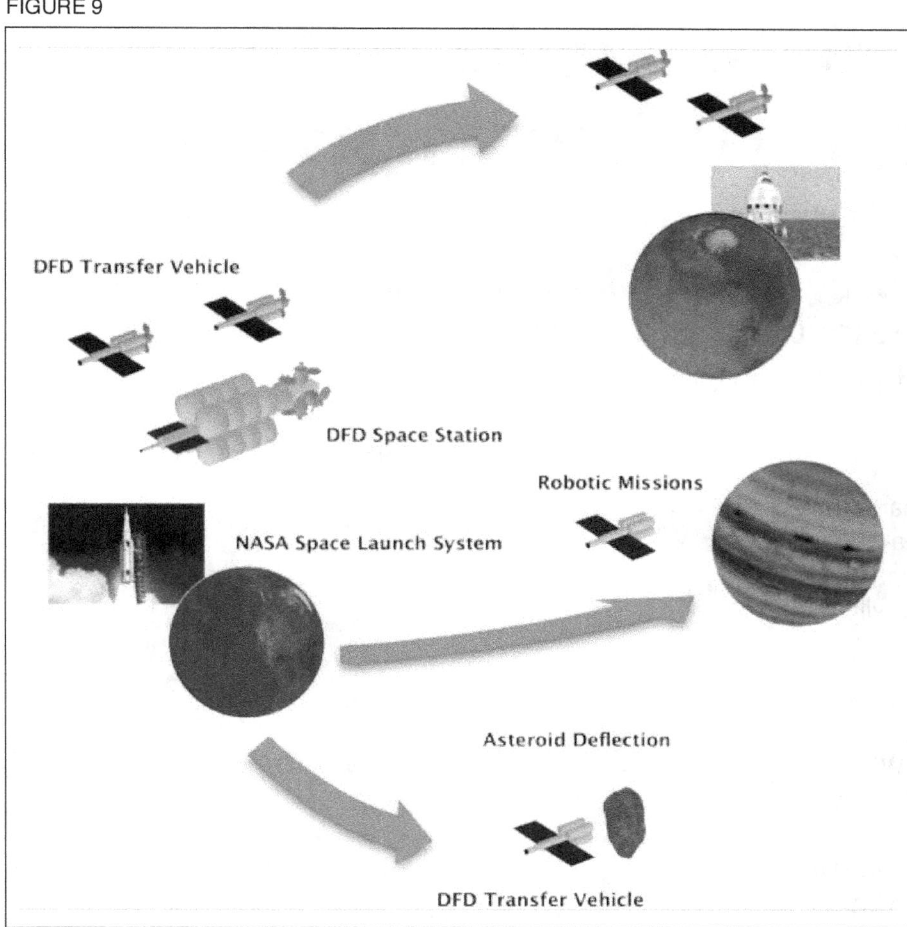

Direct Fusion Drive will open space to new avenues of exploration and rapid industrialization.

to brake, so it flew by Pluto in a matter of hours, meanwhile taking an abundance of pictures. The spacecraft had a very limited supply of power. Even though it was powered by a plutonium radioisotope thermoelectric generator, it had only about 200 watts of power, so that when it started transmitting the pictures back to Earth, the transmission rate was about 1,000 bits per second. So I think they're still transmitting pictures from Horizon! [laughter]

But with Direct Fusion Drive, you would have not only more thrust, but more electric power, something like 2 megawatts available for radio and other systems. So that an equivalent mission to Pluto would take something like four years instead of nine, and once you got there you could slow down and actually orbit the planet. Your transmission rate would be in the megabit region, so that much more data would be transmitted back to Earth.

You would actually have enough power to send a lander to the planet, and you could beam energy to the lander with a laser system, so that it could actually move around the planet, even though it is billions of miles from Earth, where you can't use solar power.

What this example illustrates is that "Direct Fusion Drive will open space to new avenues of exploration and rapid industrialization," as the authors themselves say.

So this proposal is sitting on somebody's desk at NASA, and it was put together a few years ago. By the way, I did ask Dr. Paluszek whether he knows of any work being done by the Chinese. He said he can't talk to the Chinese. Because it's a NASA-funded program, it would be illegal for him to talk to the Chinese—and he can't even talk to the Russians! Even though, if we want to go to the Space Station, the only way to get there is with Putin's okay! [laughter] … So apart from money, what we need is more collusion.

References

Michael Paluszek et al., "Direct Fusion Drive for a Human Mars Orbital Mission," August 2014. PPPL-5064. Prepared for the U.S. Department of Energy under Contract DE-AC02-09CH11466. https://www.osti.gov/scitech/servlets/purl/1182281

Ryan Whitwam, "NASA-Funded Startup to Build Fusion-Powered Rockets," June 13, 2017. https://www.extremetech.com/extreme/250836-nasa-funded-startup-aims-build-fusion-powered-rockets

Stephanie Thomas, "Fusion-Enabled Pluto Orbiter and Lander," April 7, 2016. https://www.nasa.gov/feature/fusion-enabled-pluto-orbiter-and-lander

Every Day Counts In Today's Showdown To Save Civilization

NEW REDUCED PRICE!

That's why you need EIR's **Daily Alert Service**, a strategic overview compiled with the input of Lyndon LaRouche, and delivered to your email 5 days a week.

The election of Donald Trump to the Presidency of the Untied States has launched a new global era whose character has yet to be determined. The Obama-Clinton drive toward confrontation with Russia has been disrupted--but what will come next?

Over the next weeks and months there will be a pitched battle to determine the course of the Trump Administration. Will it pursue policies of cooperation with Russia and China in the New Silk Road, as the President-Elect has given some signs of? Will it follow through against Wall Street with Glass-Steagall?

The opposition to these policies will be fierce. If there is to be a positive outcome to this battle, an informed citizenry must do its part--intervening, educating, inspiring. That's why you need the EIR Daily Alert more than ever.

TUESDAY, NOVEMBER 22, 2016

Volume 3, Number 65

EIR Daily Alert Service

P.O. Box 17390, Washington, DC 20041-0390

- Only Global Solutions, Based on New Principles, Can Work
- Tulsi Gabbard Meets with Donald Trump Regarding Syria
- Robert Kagan Throws in the Towel, Complains U.S. Is Becoming 'Solipsistic'
- War Party Moving To Preempt Trump-Putin Reset
- Syrian Army Makes More Progress in Aleppo
- Duterte Gives OK to Nuclear Power for Philippines
- Europe Will Suffer from Maintaining Russia Sanctions
- Former Chilean Diplomat Confirmed, 'We Will Joyfully Welcome Xi Jinping'
- Duterte and Putin Establish Philippines-Russia Cooperation
- François Fillon, Pro-Russian Thatcherite, Wins First Round of French Right-Wing Presidential Primary

EDITORIAL

Only Global Solutions, Based on New Principles, Can Work

WHAT THE CONGRESS NEEDS TO LEARN

The Lost Art of the Capital Budget

by Lyndon H. LaRouche, Jr.

Dedicated, poetically, to my wife, Helga, for the ominously lovely occasion of our 29th Wedding Anniversary.

Lyndon LaRouche in this article, completed for publication December 2006, warned of the danger of out-of-control derivatives speculation, which had then brought the economy "careening" toward a blow-out, "which should be, ordinarily, expected within the span of a few months ahead." The housing bubble implosion surfaced in February 2007 and exploded in mid-2008 with the now well-known massive economic dislocation from which we are still suffering greatly. Now is the time to recover: This "lost art" of recovery must now be mastered.

Since that notorious uproar of 1968, which erupted in Europe as in the Americas, the mayfly passions of the upper twenty percentile of today's reigning white collar ("Baby Boomer") generation, are frequently expressed as a loss of the desire for the practice of long-term marriages, a loss of caring for the prospects for younger generations, and a loss of any interest in investment in the future of the physical economy of other nations, or even their own. Hence, since that generation dominates our Senate and also much of our House of Representatives, our Congress had, in the main, lately misplaced the pivotal conception on which the future existence of our nation now depends: ***the concept of the capital budget***.

This must now be changed.

What has been lost, is a sense of the meaning of "indispensable capital investment in the physical conditions of progress"; it means a loss of the meaning of the investment required, not only to rescue the U.S.A., but to secure the civilized future existence of the world as a whole.

EIRNS/Stuart Lewis

Under the reign of the Baby Boomers, our Congress has "misplaced the vital conception on which the future existence of our nation now depends: the concept of the capital budget," LaRouche writes.

Some among you are perhaps angered by my saying this? Think carefully. Witness the ration of members of the U.S. Congress who count every budgeted dollar of public expenditure as outlays which must be balanced by current tax receipts. From the standpoint of any competent economist, that policy is, in effect, the practice of ruinous, sheer, inhuman recklessness in economic policy of practice.

The change in state of mind respecting economic policy, which had become widespread in the Congress during the course of the recent four decades, has become a radical change, a radical downturn from the level of competence of the founders of our Federal republic, a downturn of more than a quarter-century, in what performance had formerly suggested might be the apparent, functional intelligence-quotient of a majority of those leaders in senior positions. This was an effect shaped, to a large degree, by the stratum, from among the typical university-oriented Baby Boomers of 1968, which had launched a virtual state of class warfare, warfare of white collar against blue collar. They were, more and more, against farmers, industrial operatives, and physical-science-based professionals. Many among them were even against anything which represented technological progress in production and infrastructure. That cultural paradigm-shift expressed by the 68ers, became the cultural matrix which has dominated the downward shift in values over more than a quarter-century to date.

So, we have generations which came to love digital computers, but chiefly as a source of entertainment; they loved the entertainment value of computers so much, that they demanded the replacement of competent scientists, engineers, and machine-tool-design specialists, by the inherently uncreative idiot-machines composed to display the benchmarkers' intrinsic incompetence: we have seen, thus, the reckless use of computer technology for the attempted elimination of the role of the creative powers of the individual human mind of the design engineer in the world's economy.

Formal mathematics is not creativity; creativity is uniquely a sovereign quality of innovation specific to the potentials for self-development of the individual human mind. It is a quality expressed, not by mathematics, but by the discoveries of universal physical principles, such as Johannes Kepler's uniquely original discovery of universal gravitation, as Albert Einstein emphasized this fact about Kepler's and Bernhard Rie-

mann's work. It is the individual creative mind in Classical art, as by Leonardo da Vinci, or Johann Sebastian Bach. The suppression of the emphasis on that kind of individual creativity, produces a kind of society fairly described as an "Orwellian nightmare," a "Brave New World" fantasy, like that produced by the psychotomimetic mind of an Aldous Huxley.

So, as in our Louisiana, that reigning generation of today, swapped productive development and its necessary basic economic infrastructure, for public revenues based on public subsidy of mass gambling; that generation built casinos, instead of defenses against more or less inevitable hurricanes in the three-to-five-scale range.

That generation exported our industries to places abroad where labor was very cheap, and costs of basic economic infrastructure were chiefly disregarded, thus bankrupting not only more and more of our local communities, but also even entire Federal states. In fact, this practice, sometimes called "outsourcing," actually lowered the net physical productivity, per capita, of the world as a whole. More of the world's net productivity, per capita and per square kilometer, was actually lost in North America and Europe, for example, than was gained in Asia.[1]

Study our nation's downward plunging physical condition, county by county, since Richard Nixon was inaugurated as President. Produce animated chronological representations of even the most common types of census figures compiled more or less regularly by governments, or by standard private agencies engaged in such economic studies. See the shift in employment, from productive work-places, toward a virtually "Third World" quality of unskilled services. See the collapse in revenues of states and counties, county by county, over these decades. This ruinous trend of the recent thirty-five years, has not been an accident; it has been the product of policy-decisions made in places like Wall Street and the City of London, and imposed, from such places, upon

---

1. This would be (perhaps, "will be") evident in the chain-reaction effects of a near-future collapse of the U.S. economy. A collapse of the U.S. economy would mean a collapse of the U.S. as an importer to the world, such as Asia. It would mean, also, a chain-reaction collapse of the planet's whole monetary-financial system, unless a Franklin Roosevelt-style substitute were supplied almost immediately. The loss of net productivity through such chain-reaction effects, in Asia, alone, would lower the net productive output, per capita, throughout the world. Thus, taking the world economy as a whole, over the interval 1971-2006, the productive potential of the human species would have shrunk, in net effect, over the course of this thirty-five-year interval.

The symbol of the 68er economy: gambling casinos on the Mississippi River, which were built at the expense of the basic infrastructure required to protect against hurricanes.

our Federal and state governments, This is the trend in policy-decisions which has now driven the nation into a state fairly described, at this moment, as a national economy teetering wildly on the brink of an abyss.

Current Long-Range Policy

Over the past quarter-century, since President Richard Nixon entered office, the trends in law-making and the political opinions among the upper twenty percentile of our Baby Boomer generation, have now bankrupted our nation. Those habits of opinion are, most unfortunately, the reigning popular opinion among that part of that generation's legion of "customary voters" today. At the same time, the citizens in the lower eighty percentile of family-income brackets, who have been the typical victims of this drift, including the greater number of those not "customary voters," are, therefore, rather angry now, and becoming more so with each passing, ruinous month.

By and large, these guilty Baby Boomers did not intend to be malicious; excepting really evil cases in the likeness of Bertrand Russell and H.G. Wells, and barring typical neo-conservatives, our nation's utopians rarely present themselves as being intentionally malicious. Our upper twenty percentile of the Baby-Boomer generation, were the children, born chiefly between 1945 and 1956, born into a post-war fad sometimes called the "White Collar" generation, or known as the 1950s age of "The Organization Man." It was they who were groomed to make "the white-collar revolution," not because they knew what they were doing, but because, in their eyes, that is what they had been trained, almost as if they had been circus seals, to do.

We have now entered a state of affairs, in which, even among the more respectable Democrats in the Senate, recent legislation has driven the nation ever-deeper into a non-productive direction, and thus toward the brink of a most calamitous national bankruptcy. Meanwhile, the same legislators often delude themselves that the practice of goodness is offering palliatives of mercy to families which the Congress itself has actually ruined, as by its neglecting the defense of the conditions needed for decent employment and for protected pensions at decent levels of family income.

Thus, we hear the cry from such layers among our politicians, that the U.S. government must not make capital expenditures, except by cutting the basis for the existence of those functions whose existence depends upon precisely those capital expenditures. By such foolish practices, such misguided legislators destroy the very economy of the people whom they delude themselves into believing that they are helping. That is precisely the way in which even those we might consider to be among our many well-meaning legislators, have been destroying the U.S. economy, consistently, since early during the 1970s.

Therefore, for this very practical reason: from the standpoint of any competent historian, any competent scientist, any competent economist, those currently popular Congressional policies of "balanced budgets," are to be seen as ruinous expressions of indoctrinated delusions which have unbalanced minds, a virtual product of the influence of "social engineers" who designed the aberrant mental habits induced from childhood on, in what we call our "Baby Boomers" today.

For certain reasons, I have a special responsibility, as an economist, for pointing out such presently ominous errors in practice and belief to the members of our legislatures, and to others. The relevant generation, and also others, have become so steeped in the cumulative effects of decades of indoctrination in a system designed, in fact, to ruin our economy, that they have come to believe that a bad performance of the economy, in response to this policy, could only be the failure to continue that policy more energetically, and therefore, in fact, with more ruinous effects. The fault lies, thus, chiefly, not in the legislator's lack of sufficient information, but in the legislator's rejection of information which is seen as contrary to the beliefs which have been already ruining us over the recent thirty-five and more years to date. Like the man who persists in attempting to impregnate a plastic dummy, the harder they believe, the more disgusting the results of their performance become.

Since the establishment of our Federal Republic, the fundamental Constitutional law of our nation had been set forth as the Preamble of our Constitution. The promotion and defense of the security and general welfare of our republic, as much or more for coming generations, as for the presently living, is the principle to which all features of that Constitution are, and must be subordinated, including all amendments to the Constitution introduced since the founding, and into future generations to come.

It must be conceded, that we began as not only a weak nation, relative to the imperial power of the post-1763 Anglo-Dutch Liberal power based in Europe, but as victims of the ricochet from the orchestration of the French Revolution by London's assets Philippe Egalité and his accomplice, the Jacques Necker who played a key part, with A.R. Turgot, in bankrupting France's monarchy. We were, indirectly, the victims of the effects of the Jacobin Terror, the effects of the wars of the Napoleonic tyranny, and of the merry countesses of the notorious Congress of Vienna.

It was not until our republic's victory over British Lord Palmerston's puppet, the Confederacy, that the U.S. became, and remained, in fact, a sovereign which could not be successfully invaded by foreign powers, until the ruinous George W. Bush, Jr., Presidency. During most of the period since President Lincoln's assassination, and more so since the assassination of President William McKinley, there was a weakening of the Constitutional prescriptions for our Presidential system, a weakening to which those assassinations contributed much, and placed our foreign commerce and trade chiefly under the overreaching domination of an Anglo-Dutch Liberal financier power, a foreign financial power which also reached deeply into our own domestic financial systems.

We were only temporarily enriched by the looting, conducted by our principal debtors, the British and French financiers, of a defeated World War I Germany; but, by the middle of the 1920s, our economy was already in the grip of what was soon to become evident as the 1929 Depression.

We became truly sovereign again under President Franklin Roosevelt. Even Roosevelt's political adversaries among us were not able to challenge the Bretton Woods fixed-exchange-rate system effectively, until after the assassination of President John F. Kennedy. We were undermined by the effects of that latter and other assassinations, and, gradually, with the events of 1968 and the advent of the Nixon Administration, came the floating- exchange-rate dollar, and the other capital follies which have ruined our physical economy, and looted the lower eighty percentile of our families, more and more deeply, during the subsequent thirty-five years to the present date.

The most crucial, long-ranging fact about that 1763-2006 span of our own and the world's history, is that the American System, as defined by the legacy of the Winthrops, Mathers, Logan, Benjamin Franklin, and the first administration of President George Washington, is systemically antithetical to the Anglo-Dutch Liberal system. Our Constitutional system and that of the Anglo-Dutch Liberals, are not congruent systems, but mortal adversaries, and have been so from February 1763, to the present day.

Not only did Adam Smith write what the short title of his writing calls *The Wealth of Nations*; but, the purpose of that propaganda tract, as Smith himself declared, was to incite the crushing of the forces of our Declaration of Independence. Smith was a plagiarist personally assigned, in 1763, by Britain's Lord Shelburne, to create schemes to ruin both the economy of France and of the English colonies in post-1763 North America.

Smith was no genius, but more in the character of a caddis-fly larva, collecting pieces of flotsam from his surroundings, to build his pupal protective intellectual cocoon. As a plagiarist, Smith relied chiefly on the pro-slavery dogmas of John Locke, the brayings of the Mont Pelerin Society's frankly pro-Satanic Anglo-Dutch Bernard Mandeville,[2] the doctrine of magic projected by the pro-feudalist fanatic Dr. François Quesnay, and by that other notable Physiocrat, A.R. Turgot, from

---

2. Bernard Mandeville. *The Fable of the Bees* (London: Edmund Parker, 1723, second ed.). A modern reprint can be found in a 1988 Oxford edition.

whom Smith plagiarized much of the most crucial technical content of his *The Wealth of Nations*.

From the beginning of our Constitutional republic, the conflict between our American System of political-economy and the system of monetarist usury known as the Venetian-like imperialist system of the Anglo-Dutch Liberals, has represented the principal contending foes within the domain of modern world economy. The fact that we and the British have been sometimes allies, has never lessened the axiomatic-like difference of species represented as these conflicting two systems.

The American System of political-economy, was, in principle, a continuation of that anti-feudalist system of society founded by the mid-Fifteenth-Century Council of Florence, and by the successive steps of establishment of the first modern commonwealth forms of nation-states, in Louis XI's France and Henry VII's England, respectively. The policies of the Plymouth settlement and the New England commonwealth of the Winthrops and Mathers, provided the model background for what would become our Constitutional republic about a century later. The revival of the efforts of those Winthrops and Mathers, during the course of the Eighteenth Century, came in the form of the influence of Gottfried Leibniz in shaping the social and economic thought of those adult youth around Benjamin Franklin and George Washington, such as Treasury Secretary Alexander Hamilton, who fought the post-1763 struggle for our national sovereignty, and for the crafting of our Federal Constitution.[3]

----

3. The February 1763 Peace of Paris established the Anglo-Dutch Liberal system as the kernel of a virtual world-empire of a type modelled on the medieval system of partnership of the Venetian financier-oligarchy and the butchering anti-Semites and Moslem-haters known as the Norman chivalry. In a meaningful sense, when the Venetian financier-oligarchy lost its ability to function as a maritime power based in the Adriatic, during the fourth quarter of the Seventeenth Century, those Venetians following the pathway of Paolo Sarpi, moved north, to maritime bases in England and the old Hanseatic region from Netherlands to the Baltic. This system of Sarpi and his followers, has been known as *liberalism* to the present day. This is contrary to childishly Romantic images of a British empire as the product of a monarchy; that monarchy, since William of Orange, but, most emphatically, since 1714, is an always potentially expendable instrument of a slime-mold-like social formation, represented by collaborating and competing financier-oligarchs in the tradition of medieval bankers such as Lucca's House of Bardi. The idea of "globalization" as a liquidation of the existence of the institution of the modern nation-state republic, is an explicit copy, in intent, of the medieval system which crashed into a New Dark Age during the middle of the Fourteenth Century.

The ontological difference between the two rival systems, the American System versus the Anglo-Dutch Liberal system, is that the Anglo-Dutch Liberal system is based on the monetarist principle of usury, whereas the American System of political-economy has been premised, from the start, on what Leibniz defined as the principles of *physical economy*.

Admittedly, both we rivals each employ monetary systems. The functional difference is, that our Constitutional system uses, and regulates the monetary process according to the intention to realize those purposes which are identified by the Preamble of our Federal Constitution. The Anglo-Dutch Liberal system, otherwise known as the British system of attempted global imperialism, is a system designed and managed by financier-oligarchical predators in the specific interest of usury as such. John Locke, Bernard Mandeville, Adam Smith, Jeremy Bentham, and the Haileybury School generally, are typical expressions of the modern Liberal's monetarist system of usury.

The recovery of the U.S.A. from the disaster crafted under the leadership of President Calvin Coolidge and Andrew Mellon's Herbert Hoover, was accomplished by President Franklin Roosevelt's dumping of the pro-fascist Wall Street gang's nearly fatal adherence to the British "free trade" system. Roosevelt launched a return to the American System of political-economy implicit in our Federal Constitution's Preamble.

The Strategic Conflict As Such

The conflict between the two leading systems of today's world, the Anglo-Dutch Liberal versus the American System of political-economy, can be summed up, in effect, as follows.

The Anglo-Dutch Liberal system, as the Mont Pelerin Society typifies that alien penetration (perhaps we should say, "rape") of our nation, demands "free trade," which means the unhampered reign of the usury practiced by slime-mold-like clusters of financier bandits. This predatory onslaught is typified in the extreme, by the pack of hyenas called "hedge funds."

The American System of political-economy, defines money as our Federal Constitutional system does, as a monopoly of the Federal government. Whereas, the Anglo-Dutch Liberal system's commitment to monetarists' "free trade," defines a Hobbesian system of each in war against all. The characteristic of the Hobbesian beast-man, is the Anglo-Dutch Liberal misdefinition of

From a Productive Economy to a Services Economy

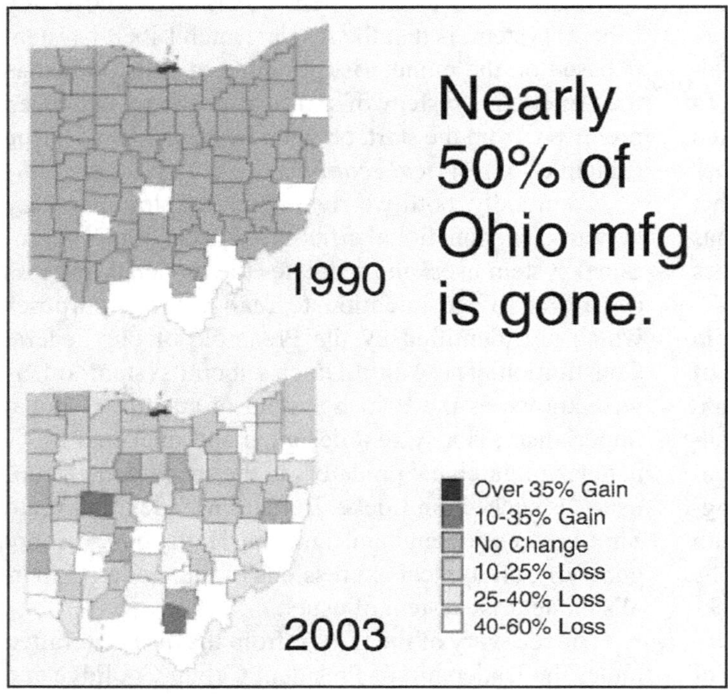

Source: EIRNS.

In the past three decades, the U.S. economy has been decoupled from the American System of political-economy, and has devolved into the services economy promoted by the Anglo-Dutch Liberal system. This devolution can be seen here on a county-by-county basis for the former industrial state of Ohio.

"human nature," which is, in fact, man as beast to man. The American System insists that the money system itself be managed to prevent the evils of the Anglo-Dutch Liberal and similarly predatory systems from operating in our republic, or in our relations with other sovereign nations, as the policies of President Franklin Roosevelt expressed this excellent distinction. (See **Figure 1.**)

Thus, our national goal, at least the national goal of our intelligent and informed patriots, is to promote the increased production of physical wealth per capita and per square kilometer. This, those of us who understand economy agree, means fostering scientific and Classical cultural modes of progress in the development of the community and the individual person. This promotion of the improvement of the condition of the individual, depends upon utilizing the discovery of higher principles in ways which increase the productive powers of labor per capita and per square kilometer. On this account, intelligent patriots prefer to promote the reinvest-

ment of retained earnings in the form of the technologically physical advancement of products and productivity, preferably as closely held enterprises under creative leadership, within local communities, as much as in the economy as a whole.

In approximation, this means constantly watching the shifts in productivity and standard of living in county or multi-county area. It means emphasizing the importance of growth of physical output per capita and per square kilometer in each such area. It means promoting physical production in agriculture, manufacturing, and related research and development, as primary. That primary emphasis requires a continually improving standard of intellectual and social life. The nation is then united by the development of the common means of connecting and coordinating these communities into a dynamic whole, that in the sense of Leibniz's definition of *dynamics*, as distinct from Cartesian-like, mechanistic-statistical ways of thinking.

Thus, for intelligent economists, reinvested earnings to this purpose and effect, should be taxed at a considerably lower rate than conspicuous consumption and runaway profits steered into financial speculation.

All in all, the system of regulation, creating a "fair trade" standard of practice, rather than the intrinsically ruinous "free trade" standard, must be reinstituted, as the "fair trade" standard was approached under President Franklin Roosevelt. This return to a "fair trade" standard would reverse the ruinous effects which the rampage of pro-monetarist deregulation has unleashed upon our poor, and now very, very poor nation, as this rampage was begun, already, during the 1970s. Scrap the so-called Liberal reforms of the 1970-2006 interval; they have proven themselves a monstrous failure.

Now, in this report, we shall first consider those points of natural forms of constitutional law, as just broadly identified, from a national standpoint. We shall then consider the application of the indicated principles of dynamics to solve the crisis within the U.S. domestic economy. After that, we shall apply that to the field of international relations.

Thus, to reach the proverbial bottom line for what has been written above, the strategic situation we face is the following.

1. Science: Redeeming Our Heathen Nation

On the surface, a capital budget appears to be a straightforward proposition in cost and financial accounting. However, the principles which underlie any competent design of that budget, are profoundly scientific, rather than ordinary expressions of financial and related accounting. This scientific complexity is therefore unavoidable; whereas, allocating a programmed loan is a relatively simple statement in mathematics, the principles which predetermine whether or not the expenditure will work out as intended, are, as I shall show here, at a later point, a much deeper matter of the actual science of *dynamics* than any customary accounting practice is able to accomplish. Therefore, to design a competent capital budget, is a challenge in the domain of physical science, rather than mere accounting. Moreover, the choice of the kind of physical-science practice needed, requires close attention to the special set of underlying assumptions which are specific to the relevant behavioral characteristics of the human mind.

Experience with the discussions of economic policy which appear from within, or around the functions of shaping and assessing the performance of the policies of government, shows us that most of the hoaxes into which our law-making processes have become entrapped, such as the Enron swindle and related phenomena, recall the case of the embittered wife telling the children, "You will not eat this week; your father, again, lost his week's pay in the gambling house which lurks on his way home from work." Such is the "fools' gold" domain of gambling, the set of shady schemes known by such names as "financial derivatives" and "hedge funds."

Therefore, this chapter of the report, will focus attention on the nature of the essential, underlying assumptions to be considered. That said, we now proceed as follows.

Americans of today are mostly heathen; that is to say, even most of those who avow a belief in God, do not actually believe in that Creator presented in *Genesis* 1, who made man and woman in the likeness of Himself. When you speak the word "God," most do not react by thinking of the living Creator of what the great and good Albert Einstein described as a finite but boundless universe in which we dwell. In practice, most, even still today, prefer a deity more in the nature of the evil Olympian Zeus of the poet Aeschylus' *Pro-*

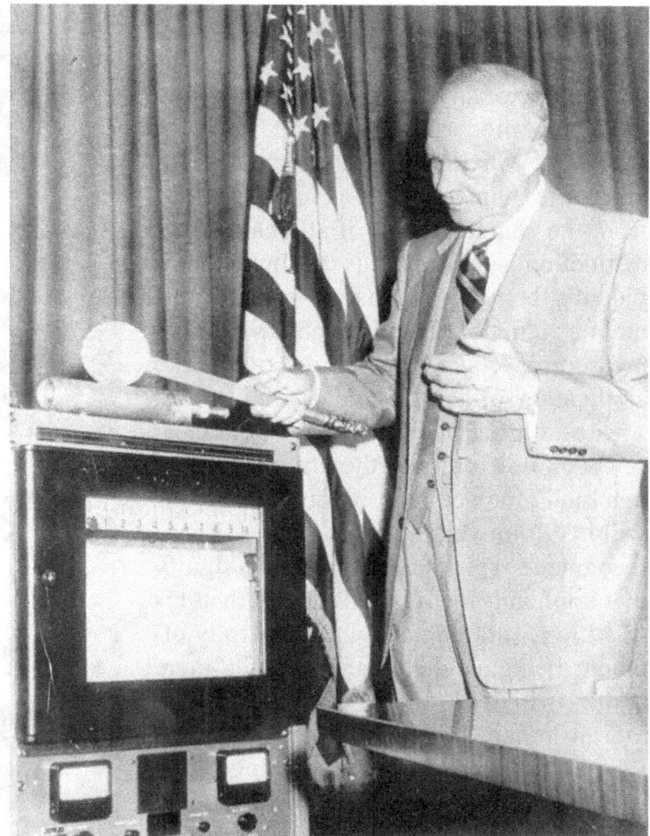

Courtesy of Nuclear Energy Institute

"[P]rogress in the discovery of the application of the principles of physical science, such as nuclear and thermonuclear science, . . . expresses the true nature of mankind's powers and assigned mission within this universe." Here, President Eisenhower symbolically starts up the first U.S. commercial nuclear power plant at Shippingport, Pa., in 1954.

metheus Bound. Most tend to believe in what such children of Paolo Sarpi as Thomas Hobbes did; they believe in the doctrine of that Satanic Iago of Verdi's opera *Othello,* the Iago who speaks of the cruel and evil, Hobbesian god he serves.[4]

That Zeus typifies a terrible oppressor who commands the perpetual torture of the Prometheus who had offended Olympus by giving the knowledge of the use of fire, such as nuclear-fission power, to mankind. Whereas, in fact, contrary to both T.H. Huxley and the Frederick Engels of Huxley's time, the human being is no monkey, no mere ape, but a creative being made with the built-in potential to be creative, contrary to the cruel law of Zeus; the human being is a person in the likeness of the Creator.

---

4. This soliloquy appears, in the second version of the opera, as a modification made by Verdi, at the prompting of Boito.

This is not fable; it is history. It is also theology. It is also physical science. It is the essence of any competent teaching and practice of modern economics.

For us who know the truth about mankind, the human mind is distinguished from the characteristics of all beasts. This distinction is expressed as the human individual's being creative by virtue of the unique nature of his living species; it is expressed as progress in the discovery and application of the principles of physical science, such as nuclear and thermonuclear science. It expresses the true nature of mankind's powers and assigned missions within this universe. This is a creativity we recognize as spiritual, saying this to signify that it inhabits the living flesh, but that it is of a higher ontological quality of fully efficient being, higher than that of a mere animal which we might eat as food. Our mortal human body is the host, and servant, from conception, of something which is so defined as the personal spiritual being which possesses the power of true creativity. This is the mission which the Creator assigns to mankind, to assist in the continuing work of universal, intrinsically, *ontologically anti-entropic* creation.

There are those confused and contrary fellows, who may worship the Sun, but hate the processes of nuclear and thermonuclear fusion on which the existence of our Solar System depends. Such unfortunates express that Luddite-like strain of perversity which has become typical of much of the ranks of Baby Boomers of the Americas and Europe, a perversity which has contributed greatly to the suffering rampant around our nation, and the planet today.[5]

John Winthrop

Increase Mather

Cotton Mather

Library of Congress
Shakespeare's Iago

In contrast to the Satanic Iago in Shakespeare's "Othello," the founding fathers of the Plymouth Colony, the Mathers and the Winthrops, believed that man's mission in life was to do good and improve mankind. Here, the 19th-Century American actor Edwin Booth portrays Iago.

The superstitious gnostic believes in a static, not a developing universe. He or she misdefines the universe, accordingly, as a universe whose process of perfection has been ended. For the gnostic heathen of this persuasion, everything is now predictable, and, for him, all that will exist is, therefore, virtually inevitable. That deluded gnostic, therefore believes, that since, in the gnostic's opinion, God must have created a perfect universe, even God Himself has thus eliminated His own capacity to modify the universe thereafter. As the beloved Philo of Alexandria and others have warned, implicitly, Satan, according to the Delphic gnostic, accepted no such lawful, principled restriction; thus

---

5. On the subject of conception of the human individual, the folly of the so-called "fundamentalist" is that he, or she, thinks like a Cartesian, viewing individuals as like particles bombarding one another in a gas system. The existence of living systems is never kinetic, but always dynamic in the sense of the term "dynamic" as encountered in the work of the Pythagoreans, Plato, and Gottfried Leibniz. Society must be designed to promote the conditions of human life. We can not change a bad society into a good society, simply one on one; we must change the axiomatic design of the society as a whole, just as the U.S. Constitutional system is morally superior to any of the relics of feudal tradition in Europe, even still today. To promote human life, you must efficiently

promote scientific and related creativity as the constitutional principle of lawfulness on which the society's function is premised.

affording a license given to Satan's faithful by the implicitly entropic, statistical laws, false laws which, like today's implicitly Satanic hedge funds, were assumed to fetter the Will of the Creator. Those who place trust in Satan's power, so, are great fools.

Contrary to the brutish fatalism of such gnostics as those: in fact, as the evolution of the Solar System from a solitary, fast-spinning young Sun attests, it is an instance of the principle of continuing, anti-entropic creation, rather than a fixed, entropic universe. The Creator's always developing, always finite, but unbounded universe, is a process—*an intrinsically anti-entropic process*—of continuing creation, a process of Creation which it is mankind's function and duty to assist. So, we now move outward to Mars and beyond, to improve the management and development of what we discover out there. Science shows us that the Creator is a perfectly creative, outgoing Being, governing a permanent reign of unending, anti-entropic creation. Consequently, our assigned duty is to perform the universal missions which that commitment by the Creator implies for us.

Our comprehension of these and related matters, has been assisted notably by the work of Russia's Academician V.I. Vernadsky's development of the proof of the distinction among three phase-space domains: the non-living, the Biosphere, and the Noösphere. These three, dynamically intertwined phase-space domains, and the principles which they express, reflect the following considerations implicit in the proofs supplied by Vernadsky, and also by others supporting the principal relevant discoveries.

As Vernadsky sums up the evidence for living systems, as during 1935-1936, although the chemical elements participating in living processes, are taken from the same domain as non-living materials, the living processes associated with the Biosphere, express a principled quality of *specifically dynamic* organization of a process which, otherwise, does not appear within the domain of non-living processes as such. Similarly, the processes of society employ the materials of the abiotic and Biospheric domains, but are organized by a *dynamic* form of principle of efficient intelligence which does not appear in any lower order of living processes.

I repeat: the empirical evidence proving the latter distinction, defines a principle of intelligence not found in the biology we associate with lower forms of life than the human individual personality. It is this higher quality of efficient intelligence, which distinguishes the Creator and the human individual ontologically from the beasts, which lack that quality of efficiently creative intelligence.

This quality of intelligence is mankind's nature, and his and her mission, as ***Genesis*** 1 stipulates in its own terms. This is the proper refinement of our understanding of the great principle lodged within the Preamble of our Federal Constitution. ***Mankind's duty is not to adapt to the universe as we find it, but to improve it in a distinctly anti-entropic way***. It is to be the agent, the instrument of the Creator, in this fashion. Our mission is to improve mankind, and the individual member of our species. This is a principled mission assigned to each of us, the mission of contributing to the improvement of the human condition on this account, and to defend the principle of anti-entropic progress so that we do not retreat to a poorer condition of mankind's existence and role, than was achieved before us.

Reason vs. 'Logic'

What we have considered in this chapter thus far, must also be restated as revealing the essential nature of the conflict between reason and science, on the one side, and formal logic, on the other. This is otherwise known as the great principle which the successor of Leibniz, of Carl F. Gauss, and of Lejeune Dirichlet, Bernhard Riemann, presents in his groundbreaking, 1854, Göttingen habilitation dissertation, *on the subject of the hypotheses which underlie geometry*. From the starting-point embodied in that dissertation, as continued through such later works as his treatment of Abelian functions, and his defining of the dynamics of physical hypergeometries, Riemann lays the basis for conquering the greatest mysteries which had usually befuddled the study of political-economy earlier.[6]

The usual, modern university student of today, grad-

____

6. Late during his life, as at the Princeton Institute, in the company of Kurt Gödel, Einstein gave further elaboration of the argument he made against the reductionist sophistries of the celebrated 1920s scientific conferences. He emphasized that the heart of the achievements of modern physical science was lodged between the book-ends of the fundamental contributions of Johannes Kepler and Bernhard Riemann. Gödel's famous 1930 demonstration of the absurdity of the fundamental premise of Bertrand Russell's ***Principia Mathematica*** (for which the virtually autistic John von Neumann and his kind never really forgave Gödel), points toward the relevant affinities of Einstein and Gödel. The conception of dynamics reflected in the development of Einstein's thinking, and the view of the principle of dynamics embodied in the work of Academician V.I. Vernadsky, are the key to the practical mastery of economics as a department of anti-entropic physical science today. The distinction between merely formal, and actually physical hypergeometries, is crucial for any representation of Riemann's work.

uates in virtual ignorance of the fact that the true principles of geometry and physical science, associated with the name of *Sphaerics*, were established under the Pythagoreans and the school of Plato, before the production of the Sophist doctrines of Euclid's ***Elements***. These great ancient principles of Plato and others were reestablished as modern science through the fundamental discoveries of such followers of the Renaissance's Cardinal Nicholas of Cusa as Leonardo da Vinci, Johannes Kepler, and their followers, such as Pierre de Fermat, Leibniz, Gauss, Dirichlet, and Riemann, all before the process of development within the life-long work of Albert Einstein. Riemann's 1854 habilitation dissertation, thus opened the door to Riemann's own founding of the notions of those *dynamics* of physical hypergeometries on which the conceptual framework

Jeanne d'Arc triumphed over a tortured death at the hands of the brutish English chivalry. "The citizen must be assisted to see his or her mortal life in terms of the significance which that brief span of personal life has for generations earlier and later."

of a competent modern economic science, as a body of physical science, as to principle, depends today.[7]

However, the root of all this can be traced to precedents akin in intent to the referenced definition of the nature of man and woman encountered within ***Genesis*** 1.

In presenting a true economic science to our citizens, we must succeed in bringing the view of the moral realities of the practice of economic science, back to the sense of personal identity of the citizen as a human personality. To understand ourselves, we must move away from the customary, petty, neo-Cartesian statistical mumbo-

jumbo of the marketplace today. It is the relationship of the mortal individual to the Creator, and to the ordering of Creation as a whole, which must be adopted as the point of elementary reference in defining the actual identity of each of our selves within the context of a living process of continuing Creation.

It is by this approach, that the citizen were enabled to secure a firm intellectual grasp of his or her personal relationship to the work of the Creator. The citizen must be assisted to see his or her mortal life in terms of the significance which that brief span of personal life has for generations earlier and later. In this way, by making a knowable idea of immortality of the incarnate human personality concrete for the informed practice of the living citizen, a sense of the immortal personal relationship of the mortal individual personality to the immortal Creator is gained. In this way, we foster the moral sense which it is essential to foster in the citizen of the republic, if the survival and prosperity of our nation is to be assured during the course of generations ahead.

The investments which must be made now, if civilization were to continue on this planet, put relatively heavy emphasis on physical-capital investments which have a projected "life span" of a quarter to a half-century, and even longer. This is a span, reaching toward a time beyond the life-expectancy of today's parents of young adults, and is, nonetheless, an investment which must be made by those living now. The only assurance that the promise of the future to the living will be fulfilled, is that the will to ensure that that future benefit, is securely embedded in the work and conscience of present and future generations. Immortality, not greed, is the only honest motive of the true citizen of a republic such as our own. This sense of immortality is not mere fame; even the individual in the relatively meanest circumstances can achieve it.

Again, immortality is not fame. Some of the dearest immortals, have lived lives heaped with official and

---

7. Riemann's work to this effect, by him explicitly, is associated with the way in which the notion of *Analysis Situs*, as introduced by Leibniz, is treated as a crucial conception in Riemann's own work. The comparison of the treatment of this notion of *Analysis Situs* by Riemann, as this had been introduced by Leibniz, impels us to recognize antecedents for this crucial aspect of the notion of *dynamics* as inherent in the Pythagorean treatment of the distinct notions of point, line, and solid, in a way absolutely contrary to Euclid's definitions. It is associated with the famous aphorism of Heracleitus, as this is pertinent to Plato's argument in his ***Parmenides***. It is implicit in Cusa's ***De Docta Ignorantia***, and permeates the method of development of the founding of modern astrophysics in the work of Kepler.

popular defamation. Immortality is expressed by the enduring worth, for humanity, of the life which has been led. If such a person were despised, betrayed, and doomed in the experienced circumstances of mortal life, like Jeanne d'Arc, his, or her worth were all the greater for that reason.

A "sane," which is also to say "trustworthy," notion of those qualities of certainties which transcend the death of the mortal living individual, partakes of the same quality of the will associated with universal physical principles. The ability to adopt a confident foresight into the future outcome of present activity, requires our attention to the notion of the distinction between ideas corresponding to experience of discrete events of sense-perception, and also corresponding to ideas associated with efficiently universal principles to which discrete events are subordinated. Kepler's uniquely original discovery of universal gravitation, typifies the notion of universal physical principles known to modern experimental science.

Those notions which correspond to universal physical principles of physical science, as also to valid Classical modes of artistic composition and their respective modes of performance, constitute the body of human reason, as distinct from the intrinsically imperfect, inferior domain of mere "logic."

The universal physical principles, as their ontological nature is typified by Kepler's discovery of gravitation as being a principle of harmonic organization of the Solar System, have a demonstrably higher authority, on account of truthfulness, than any simple sense-experiences; but, nonetheless, while they are principles whose efficient existence is conclusively demonstrated experimentally, they are not in themselves tangibly discrete objects of sense-perception in any ordinary way.

These discovered, universal principles, belong to a category of experience which Kepler was the first to define, through exploring the paradoxical implications of the *equant*, as showing the *ontologically infinitesimal* reflection of any universal physical principle.[8] This was the discovery of the physically infinitesimal, a discovery accomplished experimentally, by Kepler, which explicitly informed Gottfried Leibniz's uniquely original discovery of both the infinitesimal calculus, and his refinement of that discovery, its refinement expressed as the catenary-cued, physical principle of universal

---

8. Although, this is already implicit in the work of the Pythagoreans and Plato, et al.

The Paradoxical Implications of the Equant

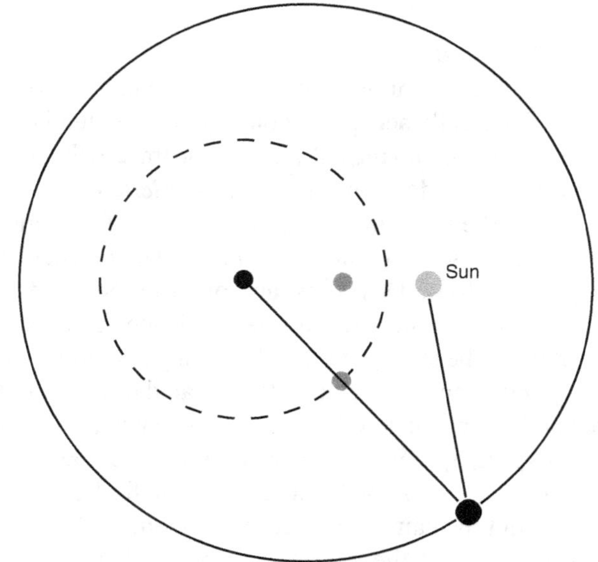

Kepler used the construct of the equant (the dashed circle) to demonstrate the movement of the constant angular speed of a planet while it maintains a uniform distance from the center of another circle as it orbits the Sun (the off-center dot of the larger circle). An animation and fuller explanation of the equant by the LaRouche Youth Movement can be found at http://www.wlym.com/~animations/part2/16/aside.html.

least action.

This aspect of the development of the notion of crucial fundamentals of modern physical science, by Kepler, Fermat, and Leibniz, most notably, is clarified by Riemann's 1854 habilitation dissertation, in which only discoverable universal physical principles are the foundations of real knowledge, and other experimental knowledge is merely subsumed by those experimentally discoverable universal physical principles, principles which are, for him, the expression of the hypotheses which underlie physical geometry.

When we take into account, that that knowledge, contrary to Euclid's dogma, was richly developed in Classical culture prior to the death of Plato, we are obliged to recognize the difficulty commonly experienced on this pivotal point, even by professionals with advanced training today. That difficulty is, in large part, the effect of the influence of those fallacies customarily traced to the sophistries of Euclid's **Elements**. Euclid's frauds against a perfectly anti-Euclidean geometry, such as that anti-Euclidean *physical geometry* implicit in Gauss and explicit in Riemann, are the most efficiently relevant illustration, still today, of the manner in which mere logic lends itself to the destruction of human reason. (See **Figure 2**.)

Euclid's Fraud

So, the legacy of Sophistry embedded in much of the body of generally accepted economy, and related law, in modern Europe and the U.S.A., is to be traced directly to the mistaken adoption of Euclid's **Elements** as the model for the teaching, and practice, of the foundations of physical science in modern schools. The mechanistic folly which René Descartes, and other modern empiricists, brought to modern European science, is an example of this. The state of mind which this habit induces in both popular and professionally educated practice, is responsible for much of the incompetence in science which spills over into the way in which people generally, and, also, many leading political figures today, think about the named subject of "economics."

Like most of the systemic errors which permeate cultural traditions, the legacy of the form of Sophistry called "Euclidean geometry," permeates, "hereditarily," a very large ration of the literate and related traditions of European culture, since the time of ancient Greece following the death of Plato. It has continued to be, thus, an important factor in causing the lack of the ability of even most ordinary people to think competently about economics today.

The proper essentials of European physical science are met as developed in what we call ancient Classical Greece. This development was expressed as a science which was built on foundations traced explicitly to ancient Egypt's practice of what was recognized by Greeks, such as the Pythagoreans, by the name of *Sphaerics*. This was the method of Plato and his school, and had also been the foundation of the less well-marked expression of the tradition passed down from Thales and Heracleitus.

To understand the ancient foundations of modern European science, we must focus our attention, initially, on the role of the principles of *Sphaerics*, on which competent forms of ancient Greek science were based, but which the concocted Sophistry of Euclidean geometry was intended to discredit and replace, then, as, later, by such Eighteenth-Century empiricists as the willful hoaxsters Voltaire, de Moivre, d'Alembert, Euler, and Lagrange. Our attention to that matter here, is limited to those aspects of the subject which pertain weightily to sources of the misguided popular thinking about eco-

nomics and very closely related matters of policy.

The best way to understand the ancient science of *Sphaerics* in a modern way, is to master, at least, the **Mysterium Cosmographicum, New Astronomy,** and **Harmony of the World** of Johannes Kepler.[9] The particular relevance of the reference to that study by readers, on this occasion, is not only that Kepler provides the reader with a rigorous way of looking at the stars and planetary bodies as we think we see them, as in the nighttime sky. Since we are on the surface of a planet moving within the Solar System, which is moving against the constellations beyond, much study and some very rigorous thinking is required, to reach the point at which the observer actually knows what he or she is seeing in that experienced spectacle. It is not sufficient to believe that that doctrine is truthful; the student of the night must live through the process of experiencing that discovery as Kepler did.

On this account, Kepler is unusually significant in the history of science in several ways, but, most immediately, in the fact that he takes the reader of his works, such as, we might hope, relevant members of the U.S. Congress and their staffs working on matters of national and international economic policy, through each step of his thinking over decades of work of discovery, so that the thorough student of his work is able to relive the actual experience of each step of those successive discoveries. It is crucial that policy-shapers not merely know some hearsay in this field, but actually grasp the conceptions as matters of principle, principles of experiment, rather than merely repeatable opinions. On this account, Kepler's written work is the best education in the experience of rigorous modern forms of scientific thinking, including the premises needed for the comprehension of dynamics, the best available in the published literature of modern European civilization, still today.

A more adequate appreciation of the implications of Kepler's method, requires reliving surviving knowledge of the methods and achievements of those ancient Greeks associated with the methods of *Sphaerics*. This is a method identified by the Classical term *dynamis*, a term whose meaning Gottfried Leibniz represented by introducing the term *dynamics*, in the course of expos-

---

9. Johannes Kepler, **Mysterium Cosmographicum** (**The Secret of the Universe**), trans. by A.M. Duncan (New York: Abaris Books, 1981); Johannes Kepler, **New Astronomy,** trans. by W.H. Donahue (Cambridge, U.K.: Cambridge University Press, 1992); **The Harmony of the World by Johannes Kepler**, translated by E.J. Aiton, A.M. Duncan, and J.V. Field (Philadelphia: American Philosophical Society, 1997).

ing the frauds of René Descartes.[10] Riemann's 1854 habilitation dissertation, implicitly, revives the principles of *Sphaerics*; Riemann's treatment of Abelian functions, then, leads toward the general principle of dynamics expressed in the notion of a physical (rather than merely formal) *dynamics* of hypergeometries.[11]

Thus, in the instance of the work of the Sophist Euclid, we are dealing with the Euclidean's reification of the theorems already developed by Euclid's predecessors, such as (implicitly) Thales, Heracleitus, and, clearly, the Pythagoreans and Plato's own immediate circles otherwise. The products of the principle of *dynamis*, which governed the scientific achievements of the Classical Greeks prior to Euclid, were maliciously reformulated by Euclid et al. as alleged products of a set of definitions, axioms, and postulates which implicitly assumed a "four-square" linear universe of the type later echoed by the incompetent René Descartes. The assumption was made by Euclid et al., that all that is true was that which could be derived, by deduction, from a set of definitions, axioms, and postulates which presumed that the universe is the solid, simply mechanical extensions of a flat surface, in which the sphere itself is, as elliptical functions show, misconceived— misconceived as if it were a product of that mechanical, "solid" extension of a flat surface.

The definitions, axioms, and postulates are never proven by the Euclideans and their followers; they are simply asserted to be "self-evident," or, as it is said, *a priori*. In effect, the Euclidean is asserting, simply,

like any modern Sophist form of academic, or other moral degenerate: "This is who, and what *I have chosen to believe on this particular occasion*."

The real physical universe, has utterly no resemblance to the Euclidean outlook and its premises.

Euclid & the New Oligarchical Model

Since the beginning of European civilization, the ancient roots of the current world crisis are to be found in a social phenomenon known to historical times as "the oligarchical model," as that model was typified by the imperial systems based in Southwest Asia. The clearly documented struggle between those systems and the attempts to establish a system of sovereign nation-states, as our American System best typifies the notion of a republic, is that traced by the poet, historian, and playwright Friedrich Schiller, as the model conflict between the republican initiative associated with Solon of ancient Athens and the Lycurgan Sparta which meets the requirements of what is termed "the oligarchical model."

The essence of the struggle against "the oligarchical model" rooted in Asia, as known to European history since that ancient time, is treated by the dramatist Aeschylus in his Prometheus trilogy, as represented by the middle section of that trilogy, **Prometheus Bound**. The torture of Prometheus, on the charge of providing mankind with knowledgeable use of universal physical principles, as this is charged against Prometheus by the Olympian Zeus of that drama, is echoed by the referenced case of Euclid's **Elements**, and by the related case of the introduction of the Cartesian system of mechanistic-statistical method, as an opposition to the dynamic scientific method of the modern echo of the Pythagoreans, Socrates, and Plato, as typified by Nicholas of Cusa's **De Docta Ignorantia**, and the revolutionary discoveries in modern science by the anti-reductionists Kepler, Fermat, Leibniz, Riemann, et al.

The Euclidean view, was given its modified modern expression, in those arguments of Descartes which Leibniz demolished with scientific proof of the requirement of the dynamic principle, which is traced to ancient Pythagorean *Sphaerics*.

The intrinsically fallacious Cartesian model, as an outgrowth of Euclid's work, assumes, thus, axiomatically, the percussive motions of abstract particles banging each other in empty space and time. To grasp the practical significance, for today, of the destructive effects of the Cartesian form of mechanistic-statistical method, as in commonplace practice of the economics

---

10. E.g., Leibniz, **Specimen Dynamicum** (1695). See the crucial Leibniz, "A Brief Demonstration…,"(1686) in **Gottfried Wilhelm Leibniz Philosophical Papers and Letters**, Leroy E. Loemker, ed. (Dodrecht: Luwer, 1989), where the famous specific criticism of Descartes' incompetence in method is presented.

11. The principles of *Sphaerics* were preserved in the school of Plato's Academy, as exemplified by the work of Eratosthenes. With the deaths of Eratosthenes and his correspondent Archimedes of Syracuse, and the rise of Rome to imperial status, European science virtually died, but for exceptions such as the Baghdad Caliphate's cultural zenith and Ibn Sina. These lost principles were revived, chiefly, by Cardinal Nicholas of Cusa's **De Docta Ignorantia**, whose followers included, most notably, Luca Pacioli, Leonardo da Vinci, and Kepler. This is reflected, most clearly, in the crucial elements of the work of Pierre de Fermat and Leibniz, as in the leading teacher of mathematics during the middle through late Eighteenth Century, Gauss's teacher Abraham Kästner. This is to emphasize that the tradition of anti-Euclidean *Sphaerics* reaches back into the astrophysics of the ancient Egypt from which the relevant Greeks derived the foundations of their own practice. It were not only fair, but precise to say that Riemann realized the principles of physical anti-Euclidean geometry already clearly implied in the work of Cusa, Leibniz, Jean Bernoulli, Gauss, Dirichlet, and others.

profession, we must return attention here, in a brief summary, to the sweep of ancient through modern European history leading through and beyond a medieval development usually referred to as Europe's *New Dark Age*.

It is necessary to treat the conflicts so defined as a matter of physical science. To understand the origins of the relevant conflict within the body of modern physical science, we must locate the source of this conflict in the persisting role of the ancient oligarchical model in modern society today. On this account, the reductionism of the ancient Greek reductionists, such as the Eleatics and Euclid, and modern empiricism, are to be recognized as essentially methods of social control intended to promote the interest of the oligarchical model of society, which the Anglo-Dutch Liberal model exemplifies for modern society now.

That connection between science and social systems, is the pivotal, global issue underlying the great, oncoming crisis in world civilization today.

Our objective in presenting this summary at this point in the report, is to clarify the sources and nature of the pro-oligarchical form of mental behavior which has repeatedly driven European civilization into great and deep waves and periods of economic and related collapse, during the course of the entire sweep of European culture to date.

To put the contemporary expression of that ancient and continuing issue into a modern perspective, consider the following line of approach.

As I have indicated above, and have presented this case in locations published earlier, the Anglo-Dutch Liberal system of usury emerged as a modified form of its medieval predecessor, a predecessor which had been the combined reign shared between a Venetian financier oligarchy and the Norman chivalry. The actual medieval system is associated with the emergence of the Norman role in both the Albigensian Crusade and a crusade usually identified as the Norman Conquest. It is the heir of the wicked, actually anti-Christian system of all of the Crusades. It is otherwise identified as the *ultramontane* system. That medieval system was driven, by its own, internal, systemic follies, into a self-collapse known as the aforementioned *medieval New Dark Age*.

However, the remnant of the Norman chivalry's power remained as a ruling force in England, in particular, until the fall of King Richard III. Although the accession of Henry VII marked the entry of England into modern history, the cultural effects of the medieval system have lingered, as through most of continental Europe, to the present day. Most notably, for the purposes of this report, the Venetian system of financier oligarchical rule, also outlived the Fifteenth-Century rise of modern civilization. It is those nasty remnants of the Norman and Venetian systems, the children of an earlier, evil medieval system, which are the core of the principal external, and also internal enemies of our U.S. republic today.

However, those remnants underwent a crucial evolution, an evolution into a form which served as a parasite-like adaptation of medieval relics to the setting of modern European civilization. One expression of this is modern European fascism, which emerged, in its germ-form, as a reflection of the Norman Crusades under Spain's brutish, anti-Semitic Grand Inquisitor, Tomás de Torquemada. Torquemada was a modern relic of the Crusader system expressed, later, as both the Napoleonic system, and the outgrowth of the Napoleonic model as the pro-satanic excrescence recognized as modern European fascism. Today, the systemic principle of modern fascism, as traced from Tomás de Torquemada and Napoleon Bonaparte's Martinist political tailor, Count Joseph de Maistre, is also costumed in such cloaks as those worn by the neo-conservatives of the Mont Pelerin Society and American Enterprise Institute.

The Venetian side of what had been the feudal form of Venetian-Norman system, also evolved in ways of adapting itself to the conditions defined by the emergence, out of the great Fifteenth-Century Renaissance, of that commonwealth form of modern sovereign nation-state which was the underlying intention of the establishment of our U.S. Constitutional republic. This emergence of a form of neo-feudalism, appeared as the New Venetian party under the leadership of Paolo Sarpi. This Sarpi is known for his role in shaping such personalities as his lackey, the hoaxster Galileo Galilei; as England's Sir Francis Bacon; as Galileo's apprentice, Thomas Hobbes; and, later, as René Descartes, John Locke, and the Eighteenth-Century empiricists David Hume, Abraham de Moivre, Jean le Rond d'Alembert, Leonhard Euler, Joseph Lagrange, Immanuel Kant, et al. This new form of the Venetian system is what is known today, either as empiricism, or Kantianism, or as such more extremely decadent outgrowths of empiricism as the radical empiricism, including what is known as logical positivism, of Bertrand Russell and his present-day devotees.

For strategic-historical reasons, the center of the current political expression of the power of the empiricist New Venetian party, was produced, as a I have said here earlier, by the latter quarter of the Seventeenth Century, as the New-Venetian tyrants of Anglo-Dutch Liberalism.

As I have elaborated on this principled issue of competent modern political-economy in numerous locations published earlier, the difference between the simply Aristotelean dogmas of medieval times, and Sarpi's New Venetian party, was that Sarpi et al. dredged the gutters of medieval life, to resurrect the figure of William of Ockham; this resurrection, insofar as it has been a putative resurrection of the original "Occam," is the root of the most significant corruption, historically, of both modern scientific teaching and practice of what passes among the more literate credulous for both physical science, and for the Anglo-Dutch Liberal varieties of modern Anglo-Dutch Liberal (and also London-spawned "orthodox Marxist") dogma in the field of political-economy.

This became what the standard of Classical scholarship would define as the "new oligarchical model."

The Subject of Modern Sophistry

The work and influence of Cardinal Nicholas of Cusa, is typified by the combination of his works in defining the principle of the modern sovereign nation-state, in his **Concordantia Catholica**; his founding of modern physical science, beginning with his **De Docta Ignorantia**; his precedent for the 1648 Peace of Westphalia, **De Pace Fidei**; and, his launching of the plan for what became Christopher Columbus's voyage of rediscovery of the continent lying across the Atlantic Ocean. These discoveries, and their offshoots, created a form of society, the science-driven development of the productive powers of labor under the modern, commonwealth form of sovereign nation-state.

In response to the resurgence of the Venetian system, which had occurred conspicuously in the aftermath of the Fall of Constantinople, Cusa's proposal for transoceanic explorations to engage other parts of the planet, outside a Mediterranean-centered Europe, led, most significantly, to the system of development in the Americas out of which the U.S.A. emerged. As I have stated the case as succinctly as possible, on various occasions over recent decades, the ideas upon which our unique form of constitutional self-government was premised, were to carry the goals of modern European civilization to what we might have hoped would have been a safe distance from the hegemony of the oligarchical sys-

Christopher Columbus studying the map for his voyage, provided by the circles of Nicholas of Cusa. Columbus's voyage grew out of Cusa's plan for "transoceanic explorations to engage other parts of the planet, outside a Mediterranean-centered Europe."

tem's relics within Europe, still today.

My late collaborator, and professional historian H. Graham Lowry, summarized the most crucial turning-points in that development of European civilization within North America. [12]

As the military writings of Niccolò Machiavelli illustrate this point, the superior power of the city and state under the new system of government, spelled the defeat of the attempts of the medievalists to regain their power, *unless the oligarchical forces made certain concessions in their doctrine of practice.* This is the significance of the influence of the New Venetian party of Paolo Sarpi. The choice thus confronting Sarpi et al. was that, on the one side, unless the neo-feudalists adapted to the pressures of scientific and technological progress, they were

---

12. H. Graham Lowry, *How the Nation Was Won* (Washington, D.C.: Executive Intelligence Review, 1988).

foredoomed to defeat. Yet, if they accepted the underlying principles of generation of scientific progress, they were politically doomed, as a virtual species of existence, by the antiseptic action of their own hand.

Empiricism typifies the attempt by Sarpi and his followers to resolve this paradox. Their compromise was, to use, selectively, certain discoveries, as the empiricists associated with the name of Isaac Newton, followed the lead of the Sophist Galileo in plagiarizing the work of Kepler, to appear wise, while, at the same time, working to castrate knowledge of the actual work of Kepler. Their Sarpian intent was to obscure the methods by which scientific progress would have an effectively independent development, such that the independent populations generally would no longer submit to oligarchical models of government.

This neo-Venetian policy is the foundation of empiricism, as Sarpi's lackey Galileo typifies this, and as followers of Galileo such as Thomas Hobbes, Descartes, Locke, Hume, Kant, et al., typify the empiricist efforts to weaken and control scientific discovery through the mystifications associated with empiricism.

The pedagogical mechanisms employed to induce that intended effect of the influence of empiricism, are predicated upon the Euclidean model's use of the defective method of a body of practice premised on a set of so-called "self-evident," *a priori* definitions, axioms, and postulates. As I have already indicated, earlier in this chapter, competent physical-scientific practice harks back to the method of Sphaerics employed by the Pythagoreans, Plato, et al. It does not tolerate any *a priori* sorts of axiomatic-like assumptions.

In competent scientific method, for as far back as we know a recognizable scientific practice, science is premised upon the notion of **universals**. The relevant notion of universals is associated, primarily, with celestial observations, especially observations which express the characteristics of astronavigation. On this account, the most interesting quality of the ancient evidence reflects adducible cycles of the North magnetic pole.[13] The deep implications of this point of reference

___

13. Young adults associated with me, have founded an internet publication entitled **DYNAMIS** (*Dynamis*), whose December 2006 (Vol. 1. No. 2) includes a translation, by Tarrjana Dorsey, et al., of Carl F. Gauss's Introduction to his 1838 *Allgemeine Theorie des Erdmagnetismus* (General Theory of the Earth's Magnetism). See http://science.larouchepac.com/publications/_dynamis/issues/december06.pdf, p. 25. This work by Gauss has implications brought out by Dirichlet and Riemann, successively.

for defining the appropriate notion of the "meaning" of "universal," were finally brought properly into focus through Kepler's original work in defining, first, the principle of gravitation for the alignments of Sun, Earth, and Mars, and, later, for the composition of the Solar System. As Archytas' construction of the doubling of the cube illustrates in a dramatic way, *the ontologically universal* is that which, as Albert Einstein emphasized, is implicitly as big as the finite and boundless universe itself, and which, therefore, is also expressed locally as a power which is infinitesimal in the sense of the ontologically existent, rather than otherwise.

This quality of experimentally premised conceptual evidence, which is associated, like the Pythagorean *comma*, with the notion of universals, implicitly defines the physical universe as composed *not of, but by* universal principles of this quality. These do not represent a perfected set of such principles, but a set undergoing implicitly *anti-entropic* developments. Any event in that universe is acting upon, and is acted upon by that universe, as Leibniz makes this point in, as referenced above, his sundry, anti-Cartesian writings on the subject of dynamics. This anti-entropic quality of the universe so defined, is echoed as the implications of Kepler's empirical demonstration of the problematic character of the implicitly anti-entropic notion of the paradox of the *equant*.

Principles are not something amid, and as if connecting Cartesian-like objects in a pair-wise fashion. They are the essential, existing matter of which the universe is composed as a universe. It is a self-developing universe, in which essential action is expressed as, or in resistance to efficient action supplied by, for example, the human individual's will. This is, essentially, *dynamics* as its experience is traced in known history to the method of the Pythagoreans and Plato's circles.

This notion of *dynamics*, is the essential subject of a science of physical economy. Human willful action in this domain is bounded efficiently by these expressed notions of dynamics for us. That means, in practice, that competent practice of economics as a science, proceeds from the whole process as a starting-point of reference, and proceeds from that conception to determine the effect of either local actions, or local inactions, upon the development of the process considered as a whole.

These immediately foregoing considerations situate the significance of Riemannian dynamics expressed in terms of physical hypergeometries.

2. The Dynamics of U.S. Recovery

The primary feature of any form of society congruent with the essential distinction between man and beasts, is the society's reigning, practiced emphasis on the human individual's intrinsically sovereign, cognitive powers. These are the powers which are, at the least, the potential which is associated with each and every individual human mind. That is the power expressed by a sovereign individual mind, a power of the universe, thus comparable to universal gravitation, which is expressed as Vernadsky's *dynamic* principle of the *Noösphere*. This is expressed in its effect on the individual human mind, but in no other species. It is expressed as the act of discovery of a universal physical, or equivalent principle, a power which is expressed as the functional distinction between the human individual and all other forms of living species.[14]

That is the specifically creative power of the individual human mind, on which any competent notion of an economy absolutely depends.[15]

That notion of creativity, as we shall consider the point here and now, is the moral and scientific principle upon which our republic's adopted commitment to long-span capital budgeting is implicitly premised.

That definition of the development of the sovereign cognitive powers of the individual mind, underscores the most essential point of difference between competent economics, based on this notion of the sovereign powers of human creative cognition, which are the expression of any true principle of individual, human personal freedom; and the opposing view, which implicitly defines a society self-doomed to a great catastrophe, unless it mends its ways in time. The opposing, latter view is typically premised upon the kinds of practiced folly which have come to dominate U.S. national practice, increasingly, during the course of the recent four, post-President Kennedy decades.

Ironically, when the U.S.A. had put men triumphantly on the Moon, the changes in leading trends of moral and economic thinking which had already been expressed by the revolt of the 68ers, had produced a culturally diseased condition which, by the beginning of the 1980s, had already caused our national economy to undergo a pathological change in reigning principle; this change was *a cultural-paradigm downshift*, a change which had unleashed a process which had been destroying more and more of the underlying policies of practice on which the original Kennedy manned-landing mission had been premised and achieved.

This consideration introduces the foremost, and the most crucial principle, but not the only one, of a science of physical economy today. This is presently describable as the principle on which the prospect of avoiding a planet-wide "new dark age" depends, absolutely, at this present historical juncture. There is recent evidence which causes us to wonder whether the elected members of our Congress are capable of overcoming certain past habits of that body, at least to the degree that the doom which past policies have now brought upon us, might be reversed in a suitable way, even at this time of impending disaster. It is that concern which must be put forward, and kept plainly in view of our consciences, lest we flinch, out of fear of misguided popular opinion, and lose our republic as a consequence of wavering, once again, in the way we, in net effect, ruined the conditions of life of more and more of our population during the course of the recent four decades.

The most significant distinction of true republics, as our Federal Constitution's Preamble itself is to be recognized, is that fact, that when that principle is actually supreme in our Federal practice, that, in itself, defines a true republic, a true republic as distinct from other organizations of society. Societies based on Anglo-Dutch Liberalism, for example, are typical of cultures morally inferior to our own constitutional order, and are not actually republics in the specific sense of the U.S. Federal Constitution. This feature of our Constitution is to be recognized as the same anti-Locke principle of Gott-

---

14. That is, as if to say, that it is an anti-entropic quality of power of the universe, which the human mind may "tap into," as no other species exhibits this potential. Clarity on this point was made possible by Vernadsky's rigorous definition of the Biosphere; that dynamic distinction of the Biosphere from the chemistry of the non-living domain, showed that a comparable separation of phase-space existed, in the function of man, relative to the Biosphere: the Noösphere. This statement reflects a similar notion which I adopted during the immediate post-World War II interval, a notion which crystallized for me during 1948, as this was prompted by my reaction to the obvious absurdity underlying the principal theme of Norbert Wiener's *Cybernetics*. My view of the connection of this 1948 notion to Vernadsky's conception of the Noösphere emerged approximately a decade later, as a consequence of my gradual recognition of the broader implications of my earlier, 1952-1953, recognition of the significance of Riemann's principle.

15. The popular, slovenly usages of language today, bestow the word "creative" on all sorts of innovations which have no relationship to the use of the term "creative" to signify an experimentally validated proof of a definite universal physical principle. Here, only the strict use of the term, for physical science or Classical artistic composition, is allowed.

fried Leibniz, which the circles of Benjamin Franklin, Thomas Jefferson's mentor for that occasion, introduced to the U.S. Declaration of Independence as "the pursuit of happiness."[16] These and kindred connections are most notable for their bearing on the design of policies of economic recovery urgently needed for our acutely troubled U.S. economy today.

As I have written in the preceding chapter of this report, the U.S. economy was founded, not on the premises of the British (Anglo-Dutch Liberal) monetary doctrines, but on the notion of Leibnizian physical economy. For example, our U.S. constitutional policy

respecting the nature of money, was already implicitly expressed in a practice introduced during the pre-1689 Massachusetts Commonwealth. Leibniz's "the pursuit of happiness," represented, for us, a concept which had been introduced to Massachusetts earlier, by Cotton Mather and Mather's young follower Benjamin Franklin, both of whom used the expression "to do good," with the same type of connotations as Leibniz's "pursuit of happiness."

Unfortunately, the tendency among our political illiterates today, has been to read "pursuit of happiness" as the embrace of a hedonistic principle. Given the ideology prevalent among the victims of indoctrination in what we can strictly define as "Baby Boomer" ideology today, the fact of the current preference for hedonism, over the common good, should not astonish us. In reality, "pursuit of happiness" pertains to the anticipated outcome of our having lived, rather than the immediate, hedonistic experiences of the living. Our "Baby Boomer" generation has been, predominantly, of the hedonist and Sophist persuasions, which, in the presently more advanced age of the members of that generation, tends presently toward expressions of distaste, even enmity against the young adults of today, young adults of the same age-range which fought and, largely, led the American Revolution and the formation of our national Constitutions, of 1776-1789.

Practically, "the pursuit of happiness" pertains to a mortal individual who lives, by conscience, in anticipation of that outcome of his, or her life, a conception of outcome which would meet the tests of immortality: "What will my life, as lived, do for the benefit of the future of mankind?" or, a child's "What will I be when I grow up?" Good deeds as such are not sufficient; we do good when we pledge to the future: "What necessary principle will our dedication promote on the future's behalf?"

All genuine development of personal moral character depends upon the considerations which enter into the individual's ability to defy the prospect of torture, such as torture intended by Vice-President Dick Cheney's policy, and to defy death itself: "Do what you will, you brutes, to my body. Falsely imprison me? Torture me? Kill me? Your ministry of pain can not take my immortal soul away! You will not make me a vengeful, Hobbesian beast, as you, for example, appear to have become!" So, Jeanne d'Arc triumphed, at a later council of the Catholic Church, and also through the monarchy of France's Louis XI, already during that same cen-

---

16. That expression, "the pursuit of happiness," was taken by the founders of our republic from Gottfried Leibniz's *New Essays on Human Understanding*. The work in which that expression was located for Franklin et al., had been written by Leibniz as an intended part of his ongoing literary debate of principles with John Locke. Locke's death held back the publication of the *New Essays* by Leibniz at that time. However, later, German circles associated with the leading teacher of mathematics of that time, the German Abraham Kästner, had caused this Leibniz text to be forwarded to Franklin via London. There were problems in the initial delivery, but the work reached Franklin later.

This work represents a significant element in the entry of Leibniz's work on politics, and from his founding of the science of physical economy, in 1671-1672, into the later shaping of those features of the U.S. Constitutional system of self-government and economic policy reflected in the work of Alexander Hamilton. These connections to Leibniz's work played a crucial, leading role in defining the U.S. Federal Constitutional system, as in direct and total opposition to the thinking of English empiricists such as John Locke.

A.G. Kästner was born in 1719, in Leipzig, thus, shortly after the death of Leibniz. As some relevant biographical details are now rather conveniently available to researchers in the work published, with Johann Ehrenfried Hofmann's foreword, in a 1970 reprint edition of Kästner's *Geschichte der Mathematik* (New York: Olms, 1970): Kästner was the son of a Leipzig University Jurist, who became, in turn, an extremely influential figure of his time, both as a mathematician, but also as an important figure in the revival of Classical culture in Europe. Kästner, who adopted a lifelong dedication to defending the principles of the work of Leibniz and Johann Sebastian Bach, is otherwise famous as the teacher and friend of the Gotthold Lessing who, together with Moses Mendelssohn, launched the cultural movement which made European support of the American cause possible.

Kästner's academic career eventually brought him, as Professor in Mathematics and Physics, to Göttingen University, where he became the host for a visit there by Benjamin Franklin. Kästner, as the founder of an explicitly anti-Euclidean modern geometry, is otherwise famous in the history of mathematics from his part, together with Zimmerman, as among the key figures in the education of Carl F. Gauss. Unfortunately, Hofmann's representation of the issues of Kästner's defense of Leibniz, against the hoaxes of the Euler, d'Alembert, Lagrange, Laplace, et al., is a factitious concoction, directly contrary to fact, as this is shown by the fact that Kästner student Carl F. Gauss demolished the Newtonians on the issues of their method, in Gauss's 1799 dissertation, a dissertation on the subject of what was later retitled as his first version of *The Fundamental Theorem of Algebra*.

tury, a triumph, thus, over a tortured death at the hands of the brutish English chivalry.

For the founders of what became our republic, who were chiefly Christians (despite the poor moral quality of some of their neighbors in the colonies and republic during relevant past times), they were seen by themselves as persons who, like the devout Christian ecumenicist Leibniz himself, held to the notion of "the pursuit of happiness," as Leibniz defined it in opposition to Locke; it was, for Leibniz and for our republic's founders, an expression of the most deep-rooted certainty respecting the relationship of the mortal individual to the immortal personality participating willfully in the Creator.

The connection of such reflections on the roots of our U.S. Federal Constitution, should be clearly seen as bearing very much on the issues of our topic of capital budgeting. People whose moral outlook does not look beyond the mortal issues of hedonistic pleasure and pain, have no efficient passion in the matter of those decisions which are the principal concern of persons sensible of the importance of their own souls. Therefore, they have no serious commitment to their contribution to the future.

Thus, people whose moral development has not risen to the level represented by the U.S. Declaration of Independence's "the pursuit of happiness," and submission, on that account, to the authority of the Preamble of our U.S. Federal Constitution, lack an effective conscience respecting the efficient realization of the future, and, therefore, tend toward the so-called "hedonistic principle." The morally crippled among us, have leaned toward the utilitarianism of the frankly pro-Satanic leader of the British Foreign Office's "Secret Committee," Jeremy Bentham. Like Aaron Burr, the New York banker who was a protégé of the British Foreign Office's spy-master, Bentham, they can not be trusted with matters pertaining to the life-and-death issues they might bequeath to future generations, to our posterity.

The truly existential crisis which has now overtaken our United States, requires intentions which rise above, and reject the passions which have governed our national trends in economic and related practice, increasingly, over, most emphatically, the recent three and a half decades. This correction must now be made among our citizens and other relevant persons. The future existence of our nation, and the meaning of your having lived, after you are gone, depends upon finding that quality of commitment within yourself.

The Case of Poor Myron Scholes

The most crucial of the practical questions posed to any thoughtful person, is that posed by locating morality in respect to the issues of the commitment of our present experience of living, that within the context defined as *the outcome* of *what we do, now, for reason of the future, rather than as reaction to the experience of what has* apparently *occurred until now.*

Consequently, the crucial question is posed by merely asking, "What is that future?"

There are two mutually irreconcilable ways of treating the meaning of "future" in that frame of reference. One, intrinsically incompetent approach, is the statistical outlook, which is in accord with the attempt to see the future as determined, as if statistically, by presently operating principles, rather than seeing the future as a change in course imposed by the onrush of new kinds of principled operating conditions. The only competent approach is that which I have presented in earlier pages of this report; for example, as the approach of the competent method of scientific inquiry which is to be traced in European culture from the standpoint of that Pythagorean method taken, in turn, from the starting-point of Egyptian astrophysics, *Sphaerics*. This I have defined above as the same method which the follower of Nicholas of Cusa and Leonardo da Vinci, Johannes Kepler, displayed in his uniquely original creation of *a systematic structure for modern physical science considered as, implicitly, a whole exploration of a single, finite but unbounded universe*.

The defective approach, as typified by René Descartes and his followers among the professed "Newtonians," is the mechanistic-statistical method, that premised on a modern, empiricist, virtually "flat Earth" reading of the precedent of Euclidean *apriorism*.

Consider the notorious incompetence of the mathematical method of the Myron Scholes and Robert Merton associated with the authorship of the August-September 1998 financial catastrophe, and the present resumption of a far vaster echo of that 1998 crisis. This 1998 development was and is a crisis based on a current persistence of the same silly system as that of Scholes and company, in the world system as a whole today.[17]

---

17. That is, as if to say, that it is an anti-entropic quality of power of the universe, which the human mind may "tap into," as no other species exhibits this potential. Clarity on this point was made possible by Vernadsky's rigorous definition of the Biosphere; that dynamic distinction of the Biosphere from the chemistry of the non-living domain, showed that a comparable separation of phase-space existed, in the function of

This experience warns us that the way in which currently hegemonic economic dogma views and prescribes for the world at large, is a systemically deadly kind of incompetence, incompetent respecting its portent for civilization as a whole. It represents the kind of corrupted thinking about economics which should be studied only from the standpoint of the relevant quality of mortician, and never permitted, ever again, to infect human life!

The morbid, statistical method expressed, typically, by Scholes and his dupes, is otherwise derived from the legacies of the Physiocrats and their Haileybury School followers; it is the corollary, in method, of a radically reductionist view of the Cartesian method. This was a method, derived from ancient Euclidean sophistries, but which had learned to speak British—or, were it "Brutish"?—at the feet of René Descartes. This is also the English copy-cat of Descartes, called "Newtonianism." In other words, the economics behind the chronic follies of the work of Myron Scholes, is a radically positivist version of the same incompetent method, the mechanistic-statistical method, derived from the failed physics of René Descartes.[18]

Real economic processes are *dynamic* in the sense of ancient Pythagorean *Sphaerics, dynamic* in the sense of the method of Cusa and Kepler, and, are, therefore, premised on conclusive proof, against the folly of Cartesianism, a proof provided by Leibniz's introduction of the ancient principle of *Sphaerics, dynamics,* into modern physical science.

Before continuing with that argument itself, it is almost certainly necessary, for the purposes of typical readers of this report, that I interpolate some words of caution here, on a relevant aspect of scientific method.

Throughout this report, thus far, I have repeatedly emphasized the crucial distinction which must be made, in the domain of mathematical statements about science, between merely formal and actually ontological conceptions.[19] This acquired habit of mine, was first developed, in germ-form, in my mid-1930s devotion to Leibniz, and was crucial, later, for both what I adduced from the portions of the work known to me by Academician V.I. Vernadsky, and in the way in which I developed a more advanced approach than earlier, to a science of physical economy which I had adopted from the starting-point provided by what I had learned from Leibniz beginning the mid-1930s.

As I have already emphasized, in preceding sections of this present report, all approaches in physical, and social science, must proceed from a top-down, rather than bottom-up approach. This approach, which I have

---

man, relative to the Biosphere: the Noösphere. This statement reflects a similar notion which I adopted during the immediate post-World War II interval, a notion which crystallized for me during 1948, as this was prompted by my reaction to the obvious absurdity underlying the principal theme of Norbert Wiener's *Cybernetics*. My view of the connection of this 1948 notion to Vernadsky's conception of the Noösphere emerged approximately a decade later, as a consequence of my gradual recognition of the broader implications of my earlier, 1952-1953, recognition of the significance of Riemann's principle.

18. The introduction of what became known as Newton into the ideological follies of the British Isles, was accomplished by a Paris-resident Venetian cleric in the Paolo Sarpi tradition, a fellow known as Antonio Conti. Conti, an avowed worshipper of Descartes, sought to find a way in which to bring a mental disease, Cartesianism, from France, into an England which, officially, usually hated everything French at that time. To this end, Conti's English accomplices selected a poor dabbler in black magic, Isaac Newton, as, so to speak, their "pigeon." (Later opening of the chest of papers of Isaac Newton, under the direction of John Maynard Keynes, revealed a lunatic asylum's worth of black magic and similar stuff, but no traces of actual scientific work! Keynes, after revealing the horrid stuff so uncovered, denounced the contents of the chest as lunacies worthy of the Babylonian priesthood—and, actually, the loan-sharking, Pythian Delphi Apollo cult of Gaea; he suggested that the chest be closed forever.) There is no proper mystery in this; the fractured forgeries of selected work from Kepler et al., had actually been done by teams, based on frauds by Sarpi's lackey Galileo, and included the toils of figures like Hooke. By the ruse of assigning authorship of what was allegedly Newton's work to a scientific idiot such as Newton himself, they had selected a person who represented no potential for uttering any actual explanations for his alleged discoveries, and thus kept scrutiny of the fraudulently alleged discoveries by Newton out

of reach of a public scandal. The principle so expressed, is that if some mountebank claims that a plastic dummy has made a great discovery, there is no danger that that dummy will say something to embarrass those who made relevant claims on the dummy's behalf. Nonetheless, it was Cartesian convert, the Venetian Conti himself, who, with the help of Abraham de Moivre and d'Alembert, kept the Newton hoax going among salons proliferating on the continent of Europe, through, and beyond Conti's own death in 1749.

19. Typical was my experience in my 1941 reading in parts of Princeton's Luther P. Eisenhart's standard text on Riemannian physics, which put me off closer examination of Riemann's work until 1952-1953, when I was driven back to Riemann by problematic features encountered in what had been my impassioned study of the often brilliant 1880s, but also the flawed 1890s work, of Georg Cantor. My own association with the role of technological transformations of the production process, "at the point of production," which had impelled me to denounce the notions of "information theory" of Norbert Wiener and John von Neumann as ontologically frauds, were crucial in my settling upon Riemannian method. My 1952-1953 reflections on my earlier experience with Eisenhart's text impelled me, then, and since, to put the greatest emphasis on the absolute quality of functional distinction between mere mathematics, and the often superficially similar mathematics whose object is primarily ontological in efficiency, rather than essentially formal.

adopted from among the relevant authorities which I had considered from over a span of no less than about three thousand years before me, requires a top-down view of the superior functional role of discovered universal physical principles, as this view is to be applied to the domain of activity to which those notions themselves are applied. Vernadsky's allotting of physical experience to three qualitatively distinct phase-spaces, including the separation of life from non-life, and human cognition from mere biological experience in general, typifies this approach. This applies, in broad terms, to the entire sweep of the subject of physical economy as a distinct ontological category of investigation. It is key to understanding development within the context of economy in general.

In each case, the ontological distinction of the physically efficient phase-spatial separation of two domains, by a universal principle, defines, and bounds the subsumed domain as a whole.

These boundaries, which define the outer limits of a phase-spatial process, are the primary subject of reference for any competent attempt at forecasting with any system which may be defined as dynamic in its relevant set of principled characteristics.

This is in contrast to the mechanistic-statistical approach of most taught and practiced, but defective economics doctrine today. That defective approach is one which seeks to define possible discontinuities of a process, by extrapolation of percussive (e.g., statistical) interactions. In the real universe, as opposed to what is still, presently, the usually taught economics, it is the boundaries of the dynamic quality of phase-space which acts upon the process, rather than the reverse, mechanical, statistical approach on the phase-space. This has been the "secret" of my personal success in long-range and related economic forecasting since my first "trial run" of this approach for what I forecast as a near-term recession, in 1956. This is also the reason why I never, since that time, make the mechanistic-statistical types of forecasts commonplace in generally accepted academic economics dogma today.

Human society, to put the emphasis in the right place, is a reflection of the human will, a reflection which includes actions of a quality absent from the animal kingdom, absent from any domain associated with the methods of Bertrand Russell's dupes Professor Norbert Wiener and John von Neumann. In society, there is no inevitable quality of consequence to be rightly associated with the usual attempt at prediction. As long as people are human, every forecast has a set of "maybes" attached to it; otherwise, without those expressed "maybes," it is simply incompetent, or worse. All forecasts premised on a "take a number from one to ten," reveal a forecaster, or questioner, who is to be compared with Kant's reference to the old quip about the one man attempting to milk a he-goat, while the other holds the sieve.

So, competent forecasting rejects what are, today, the usually incompetent opinions on the subject of the powers, and also falsely presumed lack of powers, of the human will. What actually bounds a social process, are the limits defined by the discoverable universal physical principles which are operating in that theater of interaction between the voluntary role of society and the physical universe with which society's actions are interacting. It is the universal physical principles operating as characteristics of a system, which are the boundary conditions which act upon the wills of society, and which in that sense, and only in that sense, and only in that way, define what can be "predicted," and in what way.

To restate and summarize this point, we have the following.

Actual physical economies are dynamic processes, not mechanical-statistical processes. That means, among other considerations, that a forecast is implicitly Keplerian, in the sense, both of the notion of an orbit, and, the proof of the test of the equant, that the universe is not simply repetitive, but bounded by higher universal, physical principles which give an ordered character to the evolution of the universe, or any of its phase-spaces, as a whole.

Therefore, in any competent forecast, including a serious sort of economic forecast for a system as a whole, it is the principle governing the "orbit" of that immediate system, which acts upon the system, to define a certain kind of boundary condition. As the system's evolution approaches that boundary condition, the behavior of the system is changed by that approach, which proceeds, in turn, to a limit, beyond which the system can not continue in its present form. At that point, either the system will be changed, or it will break down.

That consideration represents the presently little known, most essential feature of any system of long-range economic forecasting. We shall consider that matter here, again.

Economists With Sick, Sick Minds

There is a second ontological paradox associated with the rabid quality of incompetence reflected in the Scholes case. Scholes has merely carried to an extreme, the view of radically reductionist forms of Cartesian statistical method which is congruent with the tradition of such exemplary hoaxsters as Bernard Mandeville, François Quesnay, Adam Smith, Jeremy Bentham, and the British Haileybury School generally.

As Smith argued for the impossibility of scientific forecasting, in his 1759 *The Theory of the Moral Sentiments*:

"…The administration of the great system of the universe … the care of the universal happiness of all rational and sensible beings, is the business of God and not of man. To man is allotted a much humbler department, but one much more suitable to the weakness of his powers, and to the narrowness of his comprehension; the care of his own happiness, of that of his family, his friends, his country.… But though we are … endowed with a very strong desire of those ends, … it has been intrusted to the slow determinations of our reason to find out the proper means of bringing them about. Nature has directed us to the greater part of these by original and immediate instincts. Hunger, thirst, the passion which unites the two sexes, the love of pleasure, and the dread of pain, prompt us to apply these for their own sakes, and without any consideration of their tendency to those beneficent ends which the great Director of nature intended to produce by them."

Smith is relatively tame stuff, at least in what he was willing to expose about his inner self, when compared with that age of Walpole and the rampant Liberalism expressed by that frankly satanic Bernard Mandeville, as the legacy of Walpole is usefully portrayed for our reference today by Hogarth's elegant manner of treatment of the inherently inelegant.[20]

Mandeville's doctrine, as presented in his *The Fable of the Bees*, is that the frankly immoral must be given license in the interest of public benefits which, according to him, only corruption promotes. We have experienced this, with the help of the contemporary

The immorality of Bernard de Mandeville's "The Fable of the Bees or Private Vices, Publick Benefits" is exemplified today by the Mont Pelerin Society and the American Enterprise Institute, which promote gambling as a replacement for productive labor.

Mont Pelerin Society and American Enterprise Institute, in the promotion of sundry expressions of gambling as a replacement for production of the wealth on which nourishment and medical care depend: crime, organized and otherwise, is regarded, thus, as being mysteriously the magical source, arranged by those curious creatures operating from under the floorboards of reality, of results arranged as the outcome of the casting of the dice above, as if by the presumed magic of chance, to make some men rich, and doom the innocent.[21]

Smith's explicit precedent for his line of argument was that of the Physiocrats Dr. François Quesnay and A.R. Turgot. Compare Quesnay's argument with that of Mandeville. Correlate Quesnay's argument with Smith's 1759: "…the love of pleasure, and the dread of pain, prompt us to apply these for their own sakes, and without any consideration of their tendency to those beneficent ends which the great Director of nature intended to produce by them."

Quesnay's argument is implicitly identical to the "cheap labor" injunction of the Olympian Zeus of Aeschylus' *Prometheus Bound* against the accused Prometheus: the mere mortals, such as the lower classes in service to the feudal nobility, must not be informed of principles of the universe existing beyond the intellectual reach of their assignment to exhibit no more than

---

20. Cf. H. Graham Lowry, *op. cit.* (note 12).

21. So, in the same spirit, the wicked Galileo specialized in statistical advice to a clientele of compulsive gamblers of his time.

virtually animal "instincts." Similarly, for Quesnay, the serfs and the like on the feudal lord's estate, must enjoy the same order of conditions of life and comfort afforded to useful cattle, but have no moral claim to the product of the estate beyond that. What the apprentice of British economy, Karl Marx, regarded, credulously, as the "surplus value" generated by the Physiocratic estate, was attributed by Smith to the implied magical powers of the feudal lord's title to that estate: just as Smith makes the same argument for the magical powers of "property per se," in the cited excerpt, and as his predecessor, the putative father of the Mont Pelerin Society, Mandeville, attributes the source of public good as the harvested fruit of private vices.

Here, we should recognize the echo of that fraudulent argument by Euclid's **Elements**, in favor of "self-evident," *a priori* definitions, axioms, and postulates.

Contrast these referenced arguments from the repertoire of the Anglo-Dutch Liberal cult, to my treatment of the implications of anti-entropy, as I have identified these in the preceding chapter of this report. The power of mankind to increase the potential relative population-density of the human species, is derived from a capability which is unique to mankind, among all known living species. Hence, if we were to encounter a living species in the universe with the kind of capability unique to mankind on Earth, that hypothetical species would tend to think *naturally* as we do, exhibiting the same kind of anti-entropic power of organizing the development of its societies through the discovery and employment of universal physical principles, and would have the same relationship to the Creator as does the human species. *It would, more probably, be a representative of the universal human species as we know that species, as a species, here, today!*

What Scholes' approach reflects, is the attempted substitution of a monetary-financial system per se, for a physical economy. I had presented a relevant forecast in a graphical form of representation at the beginning of my campaign for the Democratic Party's Presidential nomination, in a public address delivered in January 1996. For that occasion, as also later, I illustrated my argument by presenting what I identified as a "Triple Curve," depicting a paradoxical relationship of rates of change among monetary, financial, and physical-economic curves for the U.S. economy (see **Figure 3**).

This figure did not present data, but the general nature of the principled set of physical-geometrical relationships among the three elements: an accelerating downward rate of emission of net physical product, per capita and per square kilometer; and, an accelerating rate of monetary emission used to support an increasing financial flow, despite the accelerating decline of physical output. During 2000, I introduced a modified version of that illustrative figure, which took into account the tendency of the required rate of monetary emission required to sustain apparent financial expansion, combined with an accelerated rate of decline of the physical economy, per capita and per square kilometer (see **Figure 4**).

Since the 1971-1972 termination of the Bretton Woods, fixed-exchange-rate monetary system, there has been a subsequent, accelerated rate of physical decline of the U.S. economy, a decline caused by the Trilateral Commission's program of "controlled disintegration" of the U.S. economy, a decline largely associated with sweeping, and deep-going measures of "deregulation." The collapse of the U.S. physical economy, per capita and per square kilometer, has shown itself most clearly, in physical terms, in the increasingly ruined, objective conditions of life of the lower eighty percentile of family-income brackets. This must be contrasted with public subsidies, as through tax-bonanzas to the upper three percentile and the health-care-management system, of apparent, but usually, morally unearned profit, such as those taken as "golden parachutes," and otherwise, in the upper-income brackets.

The combined effects of this were somewhat hidden from view by two factors. First, the fact that the physical losses to essential public and private capital-formations were either partially or entirely hidden in statistical national-income and product accounting, and, second, that the reporting on the economy by the combined efforts of the Federal Reserve System and Presidency, were frankly fraudulent, often wildly so, over the period since about 1982.

In effect, the U.S. economy had become, essentially, more and more, a financial-monetary bubble-economy. On this account, what "the market" came to assume, prior to October 1998, was the delusion that the bubble-economy was the real economy. Financial and monetary speculation in the tradition of the early Eighteenth Century's "John Law"-style monetary-financial bubbles, had been adopted as a substitute for the image of a real, physical economy.

The Enron swindle, and the ensuing rampage of "hedge fund" bubbles internationally, marked the combined aftermath of the 2000 collapse of the "Y2K" "information age" bubble, and its being superseded by what has become the presently hyper-explosive, "hedge

LaRouche's Typical Collapse Function

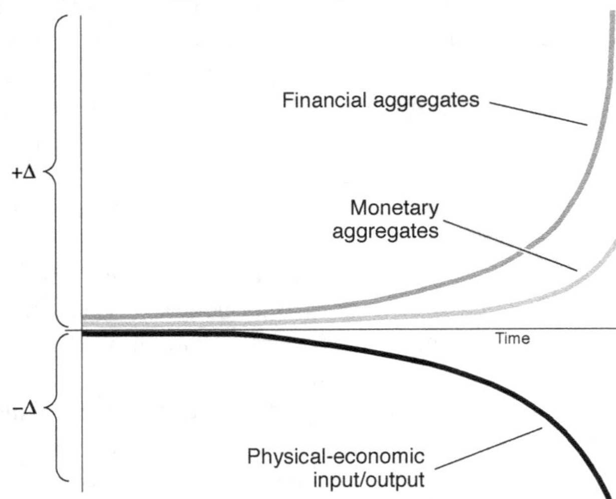

This "Triple Curve" graphic was introduced by Lyndon LaRouche during his campaign for the Democratic Party's Presidential nomination in 1996, to depict the paradoxical relationship of rates of change among monetary, financial, and physical-economic curves for the U.S. economy.

The Collapse Reaches a Critical Point of Instability

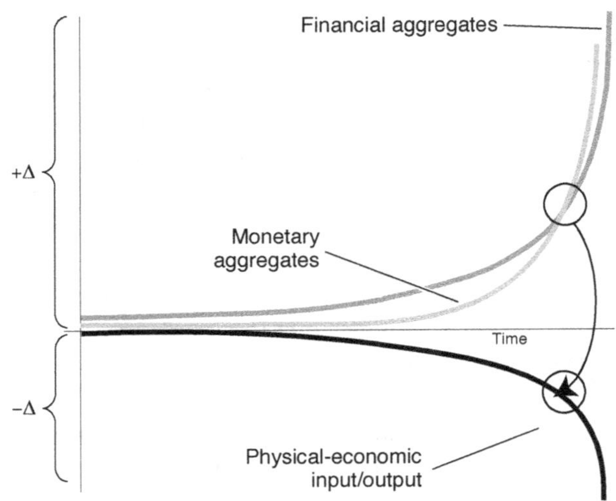

During 2000, LaRouche introduced a modified version of the "Triple Curve," which took into account the tendency of the required rate of monetary emission required to sustain apparent financial expansion, combined with an accelerated rate of decline of the physical economy, per capita and per square kilometer.

fund" bubble. The explosive state of the related real-estate bubbles of the U.S.A., Britain, Spain, et al., is to be considered as an inevitable effect of attempting to create an illusion of net growth under conditions of hyperinflationary speculation in what is otherwise an accelerating rate of decline of the relevant physical economies, that under the state of hyper-instabilities inherent in the yen-based "carry trade."

Unless there is a rather immediate, radical, Franklin-Roosevelt-style reform-in-bankruptcy of the combined international monetary system and financial system, the planet as a whole is presently on the brink of a general, chain-reaction collapse into a more or less prolonged, and deep "new dark age" of the type which modern history associates with the Fourteenth-Century collapse of the House of Bardi.

What should have happened as a reaction to the GKO bubble, in September-October 1998, but did not, would have been a general reform of the monetary-financial system then. Such a reform was mooted by President Bill Clinton and his Secretary of the Treasury, but the threat of impeachment, on constitutionally frivolous premises, impelled the Clinton Administration to back away. The difficult postponement of the GKO-speculation crisis was managed, but at a terrible price, a price reflected in the developments beginning with the mid-2000 demise of the Y2K bubble. Since the Novem-

ber 2000 U.S. general election, the U.S.A. economy has been careening toward presently impending free-fall-like conditions, with the present world monetary system ripe for a blow-out, should the dollar crisis reach the degree of collapse which should be, ordinarily, expected within the span of a few months ahead.

Only a comprehensive monetary and financial reform, of a type which could not be initiated except by the U.S.A., could now prevent an earlier careening of the world at large into a kind of chain-reaction collapse culminating in the early arrival of a planetary new dark age.

It could, and should be said, that the relevant institutions of the world at large, have either failed, or simply refused, on the wishful premises of "No! No! No! It can't be true!", to learn the lesson of Europe's mid-Fourteenth-Century plunge into a New Dark Age.

The Monetary System

The idea of a system of value as associated with a money-system, is a hoax and a delusion. Value lies only in the physical form of the economic process as a whole. However, the organization of the combined effort of the society as a unit, requires a system of regulation which guides the participating members of the society in the direction of the desired, combined, future effect. This is required, to the end of promoting the development of the process, as a whole, for both the present and future benefit of the population as a whole, in effect.

The required system of micro-management of the small, for the sake of the future advantage of the whole, relies largely on a system of credit which subsumes a money-system. The astonishing, world-shaking success of the system of regulation instituted under President Franklin Roosevelt, provides excellent illustrations of the way in which a modern credit-system may provide the means for channeling individual initiatives to the needed effect on the future condition of the society as a whole. During the 1950s, this sort of regulation in the small for the sake of the whole, was known by such titles as the "fair trade," as opposed to "free trade," system. If the U.S. is to outlive the presently onrushing financial-economic storms in progress, a return to the "fair trade" concept must be instituted now.

In other words, *the successful management of the present in the small, must proceed from an efficient comprehension of the future destination to be approached.* Society must know the boundary-condition which encompasses the present economic and related systems, and be guided by navigation focussed upon that quasi-astrophysical boundary-condition of negotiation in physical space-time, rather than by the incompetent mechanistic-statistical, implicitly flat-Earth forecasting methods derived from the failed dogmas of Descartes.

A "fair trade" system, so defined in respect to known boundary conditions, requires a relatively fixed-exchange-rate monetary-financial system. Predominantly, the boundary conditions are defined in terms of the relevant scientific principles which determine new technologies and their processes of development.

This fixed-exchange-rate rule is needed to ensure that the effective rate of financial charges on essential long-term investments in progress, must be lower than the tolerable margin of return on investment derived in the process of production and distribution of essential goods and services. For, if currency values fluctuate, this fluctuation, in and of itself, will prompt effective interest-rates and related charges to creep upward, with the effect of tending to ruin the economy at large.

A balance must be struck, in favor of physical rates of return on long-term capital investment in production and basic economic infrastructure, while allowing a reasonable charge for credit uttered by the banking and related financing systems. In other words, the standard must be set to conform to the needs and goals of a producer society, rather than the presently reigning moral and economic decadence of a rentier society, the economic decadence typified in the extreme by the former Enron and the present pandemic of hedge-fund swindles.

In our history, the needed balance has been best supplied by aid of commitment to national banking systems, as providing the framework within which private banking operates. Currently, this reform is needed to deal with a situation in which the Federal Reserve System as a whole is, virtually, hopelessly bankrupt, and must be placed in Federal receivership, under Federal management, to ensure the essential, uninterrupted, functional role of the private banking system. We can not permit a collapse of the credit system, but must actually increase the supply of carefully directed credit-issuance supplied to ensure net physical growth of productive employment and output, per capita, and per square kilometer, throughout the nation as a whole. Federal protection for the essential elements of the private banking system, is now indispensable, if a deadly, uncontrollable panic, is to be prevented.

The credit-system created to cope with the present crisis, must be a long-term system, intended to operate within a global, fixed-exchange-rate system, and that over a forward period of about two generations: fifty years. This would be established as a kind of echo of the intended objectives of the original Bretton Woods system, with suitable adjustments of design to fit both contemporary and visible forward conditions.

The global objective, as much as national objectives of the new monetary system, is to bring the level of global physical productivity up to a standard at which the system as a whole is stabilized through an assured level of continued net growth throughout the component elements of nation-state economy, and at which the level of physical productivity, per capita and per square kilometer, among the nations, permits increased and stable reliance on local systems for short-term and medium-term programs of activity. The level of physical productivity and standard of living in the constituent nations, must be brought upwards to a level of durable parity; large margins of inequity among, or within the population of nations, have the effect of serious diseases, with spreading social and other problems attached.

In sum, approximately two generations would be required, even under favorable conditions, to bring a global system of respectively sovereign nation-states, up to a level at which the carried-forward present deficits, and related defaults of the present world system could be brought comfortably under control, and resolved, without aid of further special restraints. Such is the current debt which only a happier future could repay.

The required measures of transition and development, over the coming half-century, neither require, nor tolerate repressive systems affecting the lives of ordinary citizens, productive entrepreneurs, and relevant professionals. Apart from efficient management of public and related large-scale credit, it were broadly sufficient to emphasize the regulation of the monetary and taxation systems, and promotion of "fair trade" policies. The function of the central government's role in the direction of the economy, should be the maintenance of a set of reliable and stable monetary and financial systems, through the aid of the functions of "Hamiltonian" national banking, and tariff and taxation policies; and, through the role of the Federal and state governments, chiefly, in the promotion of that development and maintenance of the public infrastructure which should represent, under present conditions, about half of the annual total capital investment in the U.S. economy as a whole.

These new directions in policies must be made now in three principal ways: 1.) Emergency action to stabilize and maintain otherwise, already implicitly bankrupt present monetary-financial institutions and systems of the U.S.A. and other nations. 2.) Mobilization of large masses of public credit at low borrowing costs, to shift the labor force's role away from low-value services employment and outright unemployment, into increasing emphasis on both physical production of goods at modern, progressive technological standards, with the related remedying of the vast dearth of essential basic economic infrastructure which has been created over the recent thirty-five years. 3.) The negotiation of a system of international treaty-agreements, covering a forward period of up to a half century, and employing low borrowing costs within a fixed-exchange-rate monetary system, with emphasis on the leading role of great infrastructural and related projects for building up the potential level of productivity, per capita and per square kilometer of the planet as a whole.

This is the true American way, which we have inherited from the founding and earlier development of our republic. This is the historic mission of our U.S. republic in service to the welfare of future mankind. This is the mission, under the natural law, expressed by the Preamble of our Federal Constitution, which our constitutional republic was created to serve in the interest of all mankind.

That much said thus far, we must now focus our attention on the broader array of essential tasks for which our economy must now be mobilized. I number these, to assist the reader in viewing the array of these tasks as an integrated single mission-orientation for the dynamics of recovery.

A. Basic Economic Infrastructure

In all that is written here, the economic policies we are considering as healthy, are premised on the conception of a dynamic system. Always, ancient Greek dynamics, the work of Kepler, Leibniz, Riemann, and also Vernadsky, are assumed to be the context in which analysis and proposals are situated. Therefore, in all that is written, the target of our attention is the transformation of the planet (and, implicitly, also the Solar System we inhabit) as composed of three general phase-spaces: the abiotic, the Biosphere, and the Noösphere.

The principal actor we are considering, is the cognitive (i.e., creative) processes of the individual human mind. The human mind, acting through living persons, affects a.) the Noösphere which mankind's actions are transforming, hopefully to a higher dynamic state; b.) Man/Society acts on the Biosphere which we are managing, and developing in its role as a Biosphere; and, c.) Man/Society is acting on the relatively "pre-biotic" processes of our planet. Our view of the interaction among these phase-spaces, is implicitly Riemannian dynamics, in which each development is interacting with the others, to define a specific physical space.

No mechanical-statistical consideration is substituted functionally for those dynamic considerations.

Our general principle for policy-shaping, is that we must, in effect, be raising the level of anti-entropy of the combined system as a whole, but we must assign preferences in the order of: a.) the individual human mind's creative processes; b.) the Noösphere; c.) the Biosphere; d.) the "pre-biotic" planet and Solar System. The principle which defines that order is the consideration that it is the human individual creative mind which drives the development of the Noösphere; it is the development of the Noösphere, which drives the development of the Biosphere; and, it is the development of the combined Noösphere and Biosphere, which drives the abiotic development of the Solar System and our planet. Such is the conceptual framework in which the notion of the dynamics of economy is posed. Man in the universe is the center of the process, which drives the role of the system of society's development within that universe.

The driver of the dynamic system so defined, is the increase of the power expressed by the development of the creative powers of the individual human mind, which makes all other contributing goals possible. Thus, the role of development, as in terms of the Biosphere and abiotic domain, in fostering the increase of the effective creative powers of mankind per capita and per square kilometer of the Earth's surface, is the reciprocal, physical-economic goal of the development of the dynamic system as a whole.

Take the illustrative case of nuclear-fission and thermonuclear-fusion-typified technologies.

The function of primary sources of power in the universe so defined as a dynamic process, is typified by what we may term, as if by crude rule of thumb, as the relative "energy-flux density" of the power-source (e.g., per square centimeter cross-section). The greater the "energy-flux density" of the mode, the higher the quality of effectiveness of the power source. Thus, fission power is superior to chemical power, and thermonuclear fusion is orders of magnitude higher than nuclear fission.

These two categories of technologies are crucial now, for reason of the increase of needs for "synthetic" generation of sources of potable water, through both depletion of fossil-water sources, and increase of both population and of current human consumption requirements per capita. There are numerous other needs. The domain of thermonuclear-fusion technologies, enables us to manage other resources, and create new qualities of such resources, and also opens the gates to qualitatively higher productivities.

The increasing of plant growth, especially tree growth, is also a general good which must be promoted because of rising human needs, and also the need for continuing qualitative progress in the physical productive powers of labor per capita and per square kilometer of the Earth's surface.

We must also consider the need to remedy functional disorders which have risen within the organization of society as in the U.S.A. in particular, during the period since the close of World War II.

Speculative financier interest has ruined the organization of our cities, towns, states, and countryside gen-

U.S. Bureau of Reclamation

Under Franklin D. Roosevelt, the U.S. built huge infrastructure projects, like the Hoover Dam, which employed 21,000 men. Today we need to make use of the higher energy flux density of thermonuclear fusion to develop new resources.

erally. We no longer have an efficient network of convenient mass-transport of passengers and freight, and have passed over from what was a relatively superior and more efficient use and development of land-area, and of management of essential resources such as fresh-water aquifers. We create counterproductive congestion in sprawling megametropolises, while imposing economic ruin, and even virtual desertification on formerly prosperous regions.

The shift into outsourcing, and replacing the closely held smaller productive enterprise with great combines, has ruined the U.S. economy, and the lower eighty percentile of our family household income-brackets, most notably, since about 1977, and has contributed in various ways to the collapse of the physical economy of the U.S.A., while increasing the financial cost of living, relative to household incomes for those same categories, and also, now, even relatively higher-income categories.

By every physical measurement of the standard of living, as distinct from clearly questionable financial measures, the U.S. economy has been ruined by the trends in policy-changes made since the latter years of the 1960s, and, emphatically, since 1971-1972. These problems were neither natural, nor historically predetermined, but, predominantly, the result of defective trends in the making of national and global policies.

It is imperative that we return to a technologically modernized restoration of the proven superior policies of practice of the pre-1966, and, in many categories, earlier dates. The better use and development of land-areas of our national territory, through increased emphasis on decentralization through promotion of technologically progressive forms of closely held enterprises in physical production, and a balanced diversity of such enterprises in each area, must accompany a deemphasis on transnational megacorporations which lack a motive of community interest in local enterprise.

Contrary to doses of mythology combined with foolish propaganda, the promotion of the highest technologies is frequently based in relatively smaller, closely held enterprises, on which clumsier, larger corporate giants depend for essential technologies. It is also a matter of service to several aspects of national security, that our nation command scientific and technological capability in depth, embedded within the pores of our society and its territory, rather than concentrated in large corporate super-enterprises which have been subject to looting by the fanged and wild-eyed, hyena-like predators of rabid financial appetites with no regard for the intrinsic self-interests of nations and their peoples, including our own.

B. The Development of People

We must create meaningful opportunities for employment. The immediate pressures to this effect are seen in the wasting and demoralization of increasing rations of our general population, especially among the poor, but also more widely. Supplying jobs as a source of income for living, is necessary, but does not address the deeper systemic problem. A nation is not a labor market. A sovereign nation-state, which the Preamble and associated features of our Federal Constitution prescribe, provides for the development of people as people, a people which participates in the maintenance and development of the conditions of life and progress for its people and territory as a whole. What is most important for the citizen as a citizen, is a meaningful role in life, a life which has merit for the benefit of coming generations.

The most essential quality of a nation, is the determination of its people to respond to challenge by mustering themselves to ensure that the nation and, especially, its posterity survive, and hopefully, progress to honorable and memorable achievements in present and future generations. Of late, that quality of our people has waned, and, among a large ration of them, what Emile Durkheim termed *anomie* is rampant.

So, on this account, of late, we have tended, seemingly intentionally, to foster a no-future outlook among the so-called Baby Boomer generation, and others. We have largely destroyed the role of the actual generation of scientific and related progress as an expression of the vital self-interest of our people in being human. Typical: we are exhausting the few remaining numbers of our professionally qualified historians. We are losing the connection we in the U.S.A., as in Europe, too, once had, to the existence of the preceding generations. We have became almost soulless creatures, obsessed with present pains and pleasures, and a vanishing connection to past and future alike. The extremes, the upper twenty-percentile bracket of the Baby Boomers, and the lower income brackets of our poor, are the most typical of the human cost which this decadence of our nation's culture has brought about.

The following, interpolated point, is supplied here to contribute a sense of concreteness to the foregoing observations on the development of our people.

The youth movement which I have fostered has two relatively unique programs of self-development. The first, is the development of the notion of the history of science from the standpoint of early Classical Greek developments throughout such crucial features of modern European development as the work of Kepler, Leibniz, Gauss, and Riemann. The second is the regular activity in developing Classical choral work from the standpoint of the Florentine *bel canto* voice-training and the Bach motet. Among the intended experiences which have been prompted by the interaction of the physical-science and musical work, is the effect of developing the counterpoint of such choral works to the degree of precision in which the impassioned connection appears between the musical counterpoint of the singers and the passion which ought to be experienced in the independent replication of the discovery of some universal physical principle.

The problem addressed by this conjunction of music and science is that students usually tend to think of an experimentally proven physical principle in "black and white," whereas practiced discipline in Classical coun-

NASA

International Space Station flight controllers monitor data at their consoles in the station flight control room in Houston's Mission Control Center during the STS-105 mission. "What is most important for the citizen as a citizen, is a meaningful role in life, a life which has merit for the benefit of coming generations."

porting passion. Thus, culture and the capacity to muster for a necessary mission are inseparable matters, in fact.

Or, as both Cotton Mather and Benjamin Franklin said it, the welfare of a society springs largely from the passion aroused in its members for the purpose of doing good. If for no other reason than to make our people, and our nation morally stronger, and more efficiently so, promote the creative passion which serves a people as the root of its proper patriotism, its guiding sense of the meaning of the durable choice of passion to do good. The choice must be the right one, and it must be motivated by the passion to do good.

terpoint prompts a known tendency among trained artists to dream in color. The connection of music and science in this kind of conjunction of the two aspects of the work in the same persons, is the much-desired reunification of scientific and artistic passions: to bring passion to science, and rigorous precision to art. The goal is to bring the two aspects of the great legacy of European culture together as one, to defeat what the late C.P. Snow identified as the two-cultures paradox in modern European culture.

The point I am illustrating by this reference, is that Classical culture, which is actually Classical to the degree it fulfills the type of purpose which I have just described, has a profound importance for society on its own account. The essential feature of the human individual, is the passion which that individual is capable of mustering for work performed as an intended benefit for his or her nation, his or her culture. A population's sense of a fragmentation of a sense of culture—for example: science without passion, and passion without rigor—tends to foster an early onset of intellectual impotence in a people. The political lesson to be adduced from such reflections as this one, is that a people acts effectively according to its sense of passion for a mission, rather than importing an emotional support for a cause which is defined as external to the required sup-

3. A Franklin Roosevelt Memorial World System

I was born in 1922, and thus experienced the transition from military service to discharge after serving my time in the China-Burma-India theater. For my case, this carried with it some special experiences, unique to me, which are, still today, of continuing relevance in the course of my successive transitions from the one status to another, during that time and the years immediately to follow. Above all of this, I have remained, always, a patriot in the Franklin Roosevelt tradition, from that time to the present. It was because of that experience, and the importance of Roosevelt to those veterans, including some OSS veterans whose secrets I came to know in later times, that I have been occupied, always, with certain features of the Franklin Roosevelt legacy, which I regard today, more than ever before, as essential lessons, essential passions of relevant circles from my own generation. This also includes my important experience of an older generation than my own. From that vantage-point, I foresee the intention which must somehow guide our presently much-troubled nation's view of world affairs today: that not only for our own nation's sake, but in the vital interest of our presently crisis-stricken world as a whole.

Most important of all these experiences, I know that the future of the world changed for the worse on the day that President Franklin Roosevelt died. I have, for example, a reliable, if secondhand knowledge of an incident, involving OSS chief General Donovan, which, with other bits and pieces from hither and yon, and some very solid evidence, too, affirms that conviction. The account of General Donovan's reaction to a certain situation, as he, late in that war, left, saddened, from his meeting with the President, typifies the knowledge which nourishes my passion in the matter; the other, historical evidence in general, lends factual affirmation to the passion.

It had been the intention of President Franklin Roosevelt, as his son reported his own role as an eyewitness, to use the occasion of the coming victory in war, to bring the British Empire and similar enterprises to a close. It was the intention, to eliminate colonialism and kindred trappings of modern history in general, to establish a system of cooperation among a world composed entirely of sovereign nation-states, nations whose freedom and development the U.S. would assist by technical assistance from the vast productive power which would be reoriented from war, to the missions of peace. Had the President lived, that mission would have succeeded; for, as long as he was alive and punching, those of us who had served abroad, and had seen the conditions in parts of Asia, as I did, would have rallied almost to the last individual veteran, at the call of President Roosevelt for this endeavor. That was my passion for our nation's role while I was back in India after the end of the war; it remains, essentially, my passion for our republic's role in the imperilled world of today.

It did not happen as President Roosevelt had intended. Winston Churchill represented a side of the British Empire, of the Dutch, and other colonialists, which had a contrary mission, and, unfortunately, President Roosevelt's successor, Harry Truman, shared in that pro-recolonizing outlook. Despite some excellent thrusts by Generals MacArthur and Eisenhower, after that war, and also other prominent figures, we lost our way, and have landed, in the end, in the awfully perilous state of affairs in which we, and other nations, find ourselves today.

Now, with one thing and another, betwixt and between, over the recent more than sixty-one years, we have come to another terribly ominous time of world crisis. In principle, in the core of the matter, we are back at the same point of decision which we faced an instant before President Roosevelt's death. The conditions are different, but the mission is, at its core, essentially the same.

The plan, as I see it now, is the following.

The pattern of cooperation among China, Russia, India, Germany, and so on, in most of Eurasia, points toward the need for a massive program of long-term cooperation among Europe, the Eurasian nation called Russia, and Asia, in transforming the partially barren, but also the world's most populous continent, into a prosperous set of cooperating sovereign nation-states. This would be done, hopefully, with the blessing and cooperation of our U.S.A.

At the same time, we are the pivot of a needed system of cooperation among sovereign nation-states of the Americas as a whole, or, allowing for some bits of reluctance here and there, most among them.

Together, we of the Americas and Eurasia must combine our efforts on behalf of the African continent, and bring the odd Aussie and New Zealander into the general scheme of play. Australia has land, mostly waste or wasted, a largely desert continent with tremendous supplies of sea water surrounding it, but we must use nuclear power to remove the unwanted salt from the relevant part of that adjoining supply of water as a whole, and to assist in reasonable forms of management of our global climate.

We shall thus bring into being a contemporary expression of President Roosevelt's post-war intention, a world of sovereign nation-states cooperating for their common security and the common good. Such was the President's intention for the United Nations Organization, and for the global role of the U.S.-backed Bretton Woods system.

The task so posed to us all, requires a bit of revolutionary effort. The world's population has grown to well over six billions living individuals, most of them extremely poor. To raise the level of the conditions of life, requires a leap in productive potential, a leap which requires energetic progress in the development and use of nuclear-fission modes of use of uranium and thorium, and the urgent development of the much more powerful means represented by thermonuclear-fusion technologies. We need urgently both of these sources of power: without nuclear fission, freshwater shortages now growing through depletion of fossil-water sites, will take a cruel toll both of life, and of the conditions of life of the survivors. Without the development of thermonuclear fusion and related technologies, we can

National Archives

President Franklin Roosevelt intended to eliminate the colonialism of the British Empire after the victory in World War II, but, LaRouche writes, "we lost our way, and have landed . . . in the awfully perilous state of affairs in which we, and other nations, find ourselves today." Here, Roosevelt and Churchill at the Casablanca summit in January 1943.

not efficiently overcome the lurking materials problems awaiting us a quarter- to a half-century ahead.

All of these problems are, fortunately, inherently soluble, if we muster the will to bring about this reform, in Franklin Roosevelt's memory.

If we agree, this, then, leaves us with some questions which require some answers. The foremost question, then, becomes: Why the sovereign nation-state?

Why the Sovereign Nation-State?

We are confronted today, especially from western and central Europe, by financier circles operating, even within the U.S.A. itself, in the tradition of Bank of England's Montagu Norman's early 1930s support for Adolf Hitler and the French Synarchist tradition. Their efforts today are focussed upon bringing the existence of the institution of the sovereign nation-state to an end. The proposed alternative from the same types of influentials, today, which is already very much in the making, is what is termed, euphemistically, "globalization."

That scheme is actually nothing but a new name for imperialism, an Anglo-Dutch Liberal imperialism in the sense of the Bilderberger tradition, under whose reign, clusters of private financier interests, predators in the likeness of present hedge-funds, are already roam-

ing throughout and looting the world, ready to drive herds of the world's already surging mass of desperately poor and homeless, from one place of wretched conditions of temporary employment, and early death in misery, to another.

We have experienced that sort of design in memories of earlier times. In one page of European history it was known as the medieval system, in which a class of armored predators, called euphemistically "the Norman chivalry," deployed at the beck of an imperial Venetian financier-oligarchy, and drove a looted Europe into the hell-hole of a mid-Fourteenth-Century "New Dark Age." The current drive, as by Vice-President Dick Cheney, is to destroy the regular military, as is being done currently with recent and continuing Anglo-American operations in Southwest Asia, and to replace military forces of governments with private armies playing a role akin to that already seen in the predatory Halliburton operations in Iraq. That "sexed up" Anglo-American folly in Iraq, is typical of the reality of what "globalization" would become: a realization of the dream of H.G. Wells' notorious fantasy, "Things to Come."

Admitted, there are still only a relative few, chiefly heavily financed predators, who wish that kind of horror-show to be played out in actuality. Nonetheless, some influential factions have a different, probably deluded dream of what they hope "globalization" could turn out to be. The latter types protest: "Is there not the possibility of a 'globalization' that would not be as rotten and evil, from early on, as we see the trends toward it moving today?" The more or less popular question we must therefore address, in reply to utopian speculations on the coming of a new, global "Tower of Babel," is: Has the era of the nation-state outlived itself, or is it that the only actually proposed alternative to the nation-state, is something at least less terrible than the frankly evil Dick Cheney's schemes suggest?

To answer such questions competently, we must, again, turn to consider some of that history of European civilization, which lies at the foundations of all that we are today.

Globalization is a new name for imperialism, the folly in Iraq today, which resembles H.G. Wells' grim fantasy, "Things to Come." This is a scene from the movie made of Wells' story.

For a proximate case in the history of European civilization itself, consider the lessons from the struggle to establish a modern system of sovereign nation-states, as Dante Alighieri, for example, had proposed in his sweeping treatment of the revival of a literate form of an Italian language. Italian, was a language older than the Latin which the Roman conquests had turned into a political form of *lingua franca* for purposes of imperial rule. The use of Italian had been influenced greatly by Roman rule, but, as the brothers Wilhelm and Alexander von Humboldt showed, did not come from Latin. Focus on the specific argument which Dante made, in his ***De Monarchia***. Then, turn to a point more than a century later than Dante's work, to Cardinal Nicholas of Cusa's design for what became the commonwealth form of modern sovereign nation-state, in his ***Concordantia Catholica***.

To understand the issues posed by the immediately foregoing set of stated historical facts, the following qualification must be stated now. As will be emphasized, in due course, the early Christians did not speak Latin, which, for them, as for those Jews who resisted becoming the beaten dogs of imperial Rome, in the sense of the modern Bruno Bettelheim's description of conditions in the Nazi prison camps, was hated. Latin, for them, was the lash of the despised, but feared Roman oppressor. The Christian Apostles knew virtually no spoken Hebrew—which virtually did not exist at that time—but, rather, Aramaic or some form of Greek, and, among the educated Jews, Classical Greek of the form in use at that time. The articulation of Christian theology occurred in the Classical Greek associated with work of Apostles such as John and Paul. More significant than the influence of nominal conventions, is the fact that the essential conceptions of Christian theology, and also the Jewish theology of Philo of Alexandria, can not be expressed in ancient Latin, for systematic reasons of the type which Cicero would have understood, reasons which I have emphasized in Chapter 1 of this present report: except as a Greek-speaking Christian theology of the Apostles impressed itself upon the emergence of a medieval Latin of the western Church.

The attempt at a Latin empire had failed, calamitously, in the west of Europe, and had been succeeded, after the Roman Emperor Diocletian recognized this failure, by a system premised, under Diocletian's protégé, the Emperor Constantine, on the literate Greek which was native to the leading Christians of that time. The imperial Greek experiment with the effort to create a state religion, as under the Emperor Constantine, provoked the Augustinian alternative, which was pushed from Italy to the Spain of Isidore of Seville, and into the realm of the Irish monks, who miraculously Christianized England's Saxons (at least temporarily, more or less), and, in turn, evoked the emergence of the great Charlemagne as the opponent of the evils fostered and spread by Byzantium. The self-inflicted decadence of Byzantium became the opportunity for the new maritime capital of evil, the financier-oligarchical, maritime center of Venice, to take over and manage the continuing efforts to destroy what Charlemagne had built. This produced the *ultramontane*-ruled system of Norman butchery, anti-Semitism, and hatred of Muslims, called "the Crusades," all of which led, fatefully into the so-called "New Dark Age" of Fourteenth-Century Europe.

With the advent of Europe's Fifteenth-Century Renaissance, which came to be centered on the great ecumenical Council of Florence, the attempt to turn Latin into a *lingua franca* of a new Tower of Babel largely collapsed. The legacy of Classical Greek science and literature, archived within what remained of a desperate Byzantium, was unleashed into Italy, thus lifting western Europe from the long reign of brutish ignorance, in the great Renaissance on which all of the accomplishments of modern European civilization since, including the birth of the Americas, were premised. The transformation of the mass of the populations of Europe, from underlings cast in the part played by the serfs on François Quesnay's model feudal estates, to be elevated toward achieving human rights, was a feat which required the fostering of Dante Alighieri's program for the restoration, in literate forms, of the language-cultures of Europe. This upshift in the rights of mankind as human, echoed Cusa's *Concordantia Catholica.* This development, centered on the great ecumenical Council of Florence, gave impetus to the realization of what became known as the commonwealth form of modern sovereign nation-state.

Those summary points just stated, in succession, bring us to the crucial point of relevance for today, a point respecting the use of language, and the relationship of this consideration to the needed defense of the establishment of a global system of cooperation among perfectly sovereign nation-state republics.

The Role of the Infinitesimal in Language

About sixty years ago, the *Seven Types of Ambiguity* of the celebrated William Empson introduced me to what was for many readers of that work, at that time, a fresh way of understanding what we ought to understand as a literate form of use of the English language. Reflect on Empson's arguments there from the point of reference provided by a leading English apostle of the American Revolution, Percy B. Shelley, in his much contested, last to be published among his principal works, his richly Classical, 1821 *In Defence of Poetry*.[22] Consider the implications of the conjunction of those referenced writings of Empson and Shelley, against the backdrop of my treatment of the implications of Kepler's discoveries in earlier pages of this

---

22. *In Defence of Poetry*, although written in full in 1821, was first published in 1840, as part of a collection of his essays and some correspondence. It is important that the appreciation of this work be situated in the context of Shelley's studies and their setting at the time the piece was written. Shelley's experience overlaps the succession and contrasts, considered in the work of my wife, Cusa and Schiller specialist Helga Zepp-LaRouche, between Friedrich Schiller and Heinrich Heine in Germany, expressed in their writings, during the relevant period of Shelley's life.

report. The reader of those compared sources should sense the aroma of a common idea about the implications of the serious form of communication of actually efficient forms of ideas, such as the discovery of universal physical principles, or the composition of Classical polyphony in the J.S. Bach tradition, or the composition and experience of Classical poetry, each and all by the aid of language.

Think now! If you do not understand poetry as Schiller, Shelley, and Mozart, Beethoven, and Schubert did, you do not know science. And, if you do not know science, as I have treated the subject of Kepler's work, you do not know poetry, or Classical drama in general. You might respond with appropriate affection for either, and that would be good of you, as far as those matters go; but, until you understand the integrity of the two, Classical poetry and science, combined, you have yet to gain a top-down conception of the implications of a functionally literate meaning of the Classical use of language. It is on this account, that I have emphasized the crucial importance of integrating a gradual mastery of the implications of the singing of Bach's *Jesu, meine Freude*, when that is linked, functionally, with the mastery of crucial leading conceptions from such scientific works as those of the Pythagoreans, Plato and his circle, as also Cusa, Kepler, Leibniz, and Riemann. Until we have located the essential principle of action which commonly subsumes both what is truly Classical poetry and polyphony, and their functional association with the Classical science of the exemplary figures I have referenced, once again, here, the human meaning of language as such remains hazy and more or less obscured.

As Shelley emphasizes in the summary conclusions of his *In Defence of Poetry*, although an inspired population may astonish historians with the profundity of its insights, that population usually does not know the actual principle which inspires its unusual rise from the dismal toil of customary behavior, to such a relatively superior moral and intellectual quality, and excitement of social life. It is the function of great poets and like-minded historians, to provide us insights into these empyreal moments of history, and that in a manner, and by a method, coherent with what I have identified as that of science.

The practical issue so posed by the idea of language for economy, is the matter of the ability of a people, once stricken with the dismal prospect like that with which about forty years of economic and cultural decline has now surrounded us, to break free of those compelling, accumulated habits of cultural self-ruin.

The change to be effected, is like that of prisoners in a just-freed Nazi concentration-camp, when they have found the gates opened, but can not seem to move ahead, through invisible gates of the mind, to freedom. When a remedy is found, the words used remain more or less the same, but the ideas associated with them have changed, in meaning and in the spirit with which the words are used. The question posed, thus, is: what is the difference?

That function of irony, in language, as in physical science, which distinguishes the creative mental powers typical of the specific notion of the human individual, is the same function associated with the process of discovery of a universal physical principle in physical science, as Kepler's treatment of the fallacy of the *equant*, in proceeding toward the discovery of a universal principle of gravitation, illustrates the existence of the apparent infinitesimal magnitude associated with the quality of action by a universal physical principle of gravitation. Such, in mathematics, for example, is the difference between a merely formal-mathematical notion of the complex domain, and the physical conception so strongly typified by the work of Leibniz and Riemann. This is the same conception of the apparent infinitesimal met as an expression of dynamics, as, for example, in the notion of the *ontological* distinction of point, line, surface, and solid in Pythagorean *Sphaerics* and in the work of Plato.

In Bach's polyphony, for example, the Pythagorean *comma* appears to express a small magnitude, which, in a practical sense, it does; but the *existence* of the *comma* is *ontological*, not metrical. Precisely the same notion of the *comma* is expressed in the role of Classical modes of irony in language, as Empson's work begs recognition of that fact, which have the same proper function in ordinary writing and speech. The essential feature of literate speech, and its echo in written form, is the appearance of the mark of punctuation which is either the comma, or a related mark, which points our attention to two or more distinct notions of substance, or actions, in such a way that the irony of that conjunction itself, when spoken in a literate manner, conveys an idea which is not literal, but clearly necessary. This distinction lies in the necessary ontological implications of the irony, not some mere decoration. This feature of literate written or spoken speech, has the same function as the expression of the discovery of a fundamental, or related physical principle in an ontologically defined, rather than merely mathematically formal, statement, which references a functionally relevant universal physical principle.

In that sense, all literate speech always reflects the whole span of the use of language or related expressions. It is the whole language, as it exists for the mind of the speakers, which is the implicit context of meaning of each relevant utterance bearing on some matter of principle. Actual ideas are expressed in this way, as ironies of what we may term *creative speech*, whose object is the conveyance of new conceptions, new ideas, rather than the simple regurgitation of the old. Thus, the domain of irony, as irony is to be understood in this way, is the expression of a process of dynamic development internal to the employment of the language as a whole.

Thus, if we permit the principle of the nation-state culture to be liquidated by the introduction of "globalization," we stupefy the affected population, driving its cultural aptitude backward, and downward toward the brutishness which the Olympian Zeus of Aeschylus' **Prometheus Bound** sought to enforce as the spiritual condition of mortal men and women. Globalization is essentially a brutish expression of what the ancient Greeks and others came to know as "the oligarchical principle." "Globalization" and "human freedom" are mortal enemies of one another, as "Globalization" is inherently the imperial enemy of all mankind.

People of differing language-cultures, may know the same universal truth, but the action of their knowledge of that truth, is rooted in the relevant language-culture as a whole, not as if in some vulgarly literal type of formal mathematical statement. Many among us are frequently challenged by fresh confrontation with this fact, as when discussion of scientific discoveries occurs between people of different language-cultures, or the attempted sharing of what is a very funny story told by the speaker of one language-culture, to the sophisticated representative of a different language-culture. Translingual puns are particularly amusing when the underlying concept expressed is inherently funny, especially as if uttered by a faithful follower of the great, greatly courageous, and amiable François Rabelais. It is, therefore, the fraternity of language-cultures, which is the normally healthy condition of mankind in general, the condition required to promote fraternity, and to promote the advancement of the power in the universe, of a cooperating mankind as a whole.

To round out the essential point being delivered here: drunkenness is a weakness, but an excess of sobriety is usually a virtual crime, especially in the practice of science, art, and politics. Simply, Classical irony is an expression of human creativity, as a distancing of the individual intellect from boredom, meanness, and a resulting tendency of these toward stupidity. All great art and science are based on an insurgent spirit of creative merriment, a state of happiness in a useful problem-solving mission, a perception that a folly is inherently ridiculous, and that pompous creatures tend to behave like that of which honest donkeys would be sadly ashamed to see in a human being. Irony is incipient laughter, an expression of creative joy in being part of mankind. Excessively sober men and women are not to be trusted. To be happy, even laughing lovingly in the face of death, is to be good. Abraham Kästner's student and friend, Gotthold Lessing, would have agreed.

The Tower of Babel, like that of Pisa, was always, as now, a bad idea.

The Essential Cooperation

The touching of the Moon, and the increasingly sophisticated exploration of some ironical features of the Mars landscape, typify experiences which have given us an increasingly, emotionally and intellectually disturbing, retrospective view of Earth as a whole. The problem here, is of a type similar to that conflict in outlook, between the commonplace economic forecaster who projects his estimate of a future time as a mechanical-statistical extrapolation, and my view, which locates the observed sequence of events from the standpoint of the impact of the relevant boundary-condition being approached, in predetermining how the future shapes the optional choices of outcomes for the present developments in progress now.

So, in the astrophysics developed through the mercy of Kepler, as we see the Solar System today, so we must look, as if backwards from the future, to a unified, and unifying conception of the options for development of the whole complex of what should be the respectively sovereign cultures of Earth. We must see mankind as if with God's eyes. You wish to be in the Creator's image;

On the shoulders of Kepler and Cusa, we must develop the next two generations of citizens into a mission for "the common aims of mankind." With the aid of nuclear- and fusion-powered rockets, we can work with other nations to develop the Solar System. Here, NASA's Mars rover successfully leaves its lander on Jan. 31, 2004, ready to provide man with more detailed knowledge of the planet.

accept the challenge of seeing yourself as the Creator of our anti-entropically developing universe does.

We must define a common mission within, at least, the range of the inner planets and related body of our Solar System, and think of the self-development, and other developments needed to bring the various nations into a condition where each is prepared for some national mission within a well-composed division of labors among the nations of the planet as a whole. We must, in that sense, work separately, but in cooperation, to common aims and ends.

For that purpose, we must return to the subject of the work of Johannes Kepler. Kepler, the avowed student of Nicholas of Cusa and, in a lesser, but important respect, also Leonardo da Vinci, lunged to create competent modern astrophysics, out of the varied kinds of critical failures of notable predecessors such as Copernicus and Tycho Brahe. Modern civilization is not a product of a Copernican Revolution, but of the leading work of Nicholas of Cusa and his follower Johannes Kepler. Cusa defined principle; Kepler discovered the principle which makes the Solar System work, where all attempts by others had failed to grasp the crucial element of solution for this challenge.

We must focus on using the progressive development of the two adult generations (of approximately twenty-five years, each), of which the first is now in motion, to bring the development of the populations and their settings into, not a state of "globalization," but approximate parity in their ability to participate in what the late scientist Edward Teller, once named "the common aims of mankind." A kind of benchmark for that objective is implicit in the obvious roles of nuclear fission and the region of work associated with thermonuclear fusion, which will dominate the development of any culture of the planet which avoids the immediate threat of a descent into what is at least a catastrophic form of planetary dark age, as we associate those terms with the decline of the Roman Empire in the West.

If civilization escapes the present threat of an early plunge into a planetary new dark age, the next two generations, that now entered into adulthood, and its successor, will manage more and more of the planet's affairs for the remainder of that new century we have recently entered. The implications of both exploration of relatively nearby space, and of a range of technologies congruent with the implications of thermonuclear fusion, and beyond, will be the vision which will dominate the successful passage through that century. If we review the history of European civilization and its outgrowths since a half-millennium ago, especially the internal development of crucial sorts of fundamental discoveries in physical science, we can imagine a point of future reference, from a point outside the Solar System, from which to consider, that in a fully rational way, the future boundary conditions which will shape, more and more, the needed development of life on Earth as a whole.

The most important thing about this view, from where we sit in history today, is to adopt this way of thinking, more than hoping to secure detailed elaboration of answers to the questions such a view employs. The crucial thing, is to beware of our adopting policies which are stupid from the standpoint of those general considerations. Essentially, we must think of building up the potential of the planet, as potential is expressed by the quality of development of the coming generations, of the basic economic infrastructure of each nation, and of the planet. We must consider, thus, the need to change the way we have come to think, as nations, during the recent two generations. We must change the way most of our people have come to think of the needs of the future two generations, and no less than that. We must come to accept, now, the implied responsibility of ensuring an anti-entropic characteristic of the development of the practice of the planet's human population considered as a whole.

If what is necessary appears to be impossible, then make it happen!

We can not get away from the boundary conditions of specific cultures which define the necessary autonomy of the national cultures of which the planet as a whole is composed. Yet, it is not those differences which should define planetary goals, or the perspectives for internal development of the respective sovereign nations. Rather, the necessary goals must be effectively served in common, despite the fact that certain differences among national cultures are expressions of those nations' required, separate sovereignties. Typical of this challenge, is the unavoidable fact, that the issue of the broad development and applications of nuclear-fission and thermonuclear-fusion technologies are necessary practically, and therefore morally, for all humanity, and all nations. Some differences of opinion are legitimate, while others are intolerable: we must know the actual differences which define that distinction.

This touchy point arising in some people's notion of the function of sovereignty, is resolved by reflection on the essential role of truth as the measure of reason. Our duty as a U.S. republic, is not to dictate what is called "truth" to other nations; certainly, the performance of the present U.S. Administration does not warrant awarding it the privilege of dictating "regime change." The authority of truth begins with our imposing it upon ourselves, which is the first, indispensable step toward the acceptance of truth by others.

We must choose the mission-orientation we assign to ourselves, to our republic. Then, when we have done that, we must tell other nations what we have done, and proffer the opportunity for their cooperation with us. Without reasonable objections, we have the finest Constitution ever crafted for any republic; it has served us well, each time we have served it well. In historical fact, there exists no rational evidence to the contrary, since we emerged as a world power, with the victory over the Confederacy project of imperial Britain's Lord Palmerston. Our Constitution was crafted as a distillation of all of European civilization's experience up to that time, since, literally, the constitutional poem of Solon. As President Franklin Roosevelt's performance shows, the world at large was mostly disposed to accept our policy for global post-war reconstruction of relations among sovereign states, had we, ourselves, not betrayed the commitment which that President had represented.

The world today could not escape the onrushing threat of a planetary general breakdown-crisis, without our providing the crucial initiative around which the rational governments of the world would quickly rally, out of no more remote motive than a frank perception of their own urgent and desperate immediate interest in survival as nations. No present government of western and central Europe could do this, nor of Asia, nor of other parts of the Americas. Herein lies our national mission on behalf of the rightly sovereign nations of humanity as a whole.

Above all else, we will not build an empire, nor will we tolerate a new one, even of our own making, on this planet. It is in the nature of what we were crafted to become, in the establishment of European colonies, as places of refuge from oligarchical Europe in North America, places made according to the nature of our Federal Constitution's principles, that we abhor any form of empire on this planet, by any national or other form of power, including our own. What we need is a world of neighbors, and a policy which states that we shall defend, with all our might, the right of every people of this planet to enjoy the same freedom.

However, to accomplish that, we must change our ways; to became, again, as under the leadership of President Franklin Roosevelt: wise enough to represent that policy effectively.

4. This Session's Legislative Effort

As the new Congress comes into its opening session on January 4, 2007, there are many postponed tasks to be accomplished, many of which must be done as quickly as possible. The central issue among all of these, is the pivotal issue of defining and instituting the needed forms of U.S. capital budget.

Without that form of capital budgeting, our republic would not now survive.

The principle governing the design and application of a true capital budget, is a reflection of the principles of physical economy, rather than of a monetary system as such. Although this practice of capital budgeting has been incorporated into accounting practice elsewhere, especially in past times, the controlling principle is essentially one bearing a U.S. hallmark. This practice was standard management and investment thinking in the

U.S.A. itself, since 1861,[23] until the rabid fit of "deregulation" launched on the initiative of the reforms introduced by the Trilateral Commission, headed by Carter Administration National Security Advisor Zbigniew Brzezinski.[24]

Notably, to make the technical issue clear, it must be emphasized that this radical, and ruinous, change in U.S. policy, under the Trilateral Commission, reflected Brzezinski's late 1960s advocacy of the shift of the U.S. economy from its traditional economic practices into the fantasy-world of "information theory" and "artificial intelligence" presented as Brzezinski's notion of a "technetronic" age.[25]

On this same account, it should be added, that, by 1982, with the passing of the frankly wild-eyed Kemp-Roth legislation, and wildly radical hoaxes concocted by the Federal Reserve System and the annual White House reporting on the economy, virtually the last shreds of economic sanity were in flight from both prevailing Federal doctrine and general tax and investment practice.

Soviet General Secretary Yuri Andropov's refusal to discuss President Ronald Reagan's March 23, 1983 proffer of a Strategic Defense Initiative (SDI), not only foredoomed the subsequent collapse of the Soviet economy, but removed virtually the last chance for bringing

23. The inauguration of President Abraham Lincoln brought what were essentially the agro-industrial and social features of the American System doctrines of Henry A. Carey into U.S. Federal practice, the same policies which Carey personally introduced to Chancellor Bismarck's Germany in the late 1870s, and, indirectly, to Japan. These were the same policies which Mendeleyev carried from the 1876 Philadelphia Centennial Exhibition to Czar Alexander III's Russia. Although the policies had been built into the U.S. republic, by Franklin, Alexander Hamilton, and others, the setbacks to U.S. strategic interests by the French Revolution and Napoleonic wars, and the advent of Wall Street pawn of Martin van Buren of land-bank-scam notoriety, Andrew Jackson, into the Presidency, postponed the consolidation of the economic policies of the U.S. Constitutional system until the developments under President Lincoln.

24. The New York Council on Foreign Relations' 1975-1976 *Project for the 1980s* (New York: Magraw-Hill, 1977), was a project co-supervised by the Trilateral Commission, notably the Commission's former director (1973-1976), Carter National Security Advisor Zbigniew Brzezinski; Secretary of State Cyrus Vance; and Miriam Camp.

25. Brzezinski was the author of *Between Two Ages: America's Role in the Technetronic Era* (New York: Viking Press, 1970), and *International Politics in the Technetronic Era* (Tokyo: Sophia University, 1971). Addressing the stresses that were emerging in the shift from the "industrial era" to an era of services, automation, and cybernetics, he wrote in the 1970 volume that the Technetronic Revolution is beginning to fracture the nation-state into "a global city—a nervous, agitated, tense, and fragmented web of interdependent relations."

EIRNS/Dan Sturman

The central issue before the new Congress is to define and institute the needed forms of a U.S. capital budget, based on physical economy, rather than a monetary system as such. This means dumping the reforms introduced by the Carter Administration's Zbigniew Brzezinski and his Trilateral Commission. Brzezinski is shown here at the Democrats' Center for American Progress in March 2006.

about the shift of the U.S., back to that science-driver form of national economic priority which would have tended to reverse the prevalent economic and related lunacies of the 1970s.[26]

As its reward for those indicated mistakes in national policy, our republic has suffered much, especially the lower eighty percentile of our households, with the immediate prospect of much worse soon, for all of our households. Without a shift back to what a return to a U.S. capital budgeting policy and practice requires and

____

26. I can report, as a significant insider in these developments, that this change would have been conducted not only in the U.S.A., but in much of western and central continental Europe, too. When Andropov flatly rejected even official discussion with President Reagan, not only was Andropov virtually doomed, but the U.S. opponents of SDI went promptly after my neck, leading to a certain unpleasantness experienced by me and my associates, in both the U.S.A. and Europe, most emphatically, from Spring 1983 until the present day. Real history is often like that.

implies, there is no hope for the preservation of our republic over the period ahead, and there would be the assured doom of a planetary New Dark Age for the Eurasian continent. Folly has run its course, too long to be tolerated any longer. It is time for the U.S. Congress, among others, to be suddenly awakened to the realities of the present global situation.

That much said on background, now to the core of the matter of capital budgeting:

The portion of an investment which may be regarded as consumed within a fiscal year, is the portion which corresponds to the part of an investment which has been used up *physically*. We must not count the balance of investment, after deducting what is used up in the relevant current year, as a current cost. Accordingly, counting Federal outlays for capital projects of several years span, all in the same year the outlay for that project is authorized, represents a case of gross incompetence in judgment, and a source of potential catastrophes if such misguided practices as that are continued. In fact, if we continue to act, presently, as if Federal funds allotted for capital improvements in the public or private sector were self-evidently current expenses, our national economy were already doomed to experience something far worse than an economic depression, a general collapse like that which medieval Europe experienced as a "New Dark Age."

What we must do now, is increase the credit uttered by the Federal government, the only agency allowed to do so under our Constitutional system, such that the total amount allotted in each coming year immediately ahead, vastly exceeds the amount used up during the relevant, current fiscal year. This is clearly a tricky business, but an indispensable one, and represents a chore which we must perform, as I can hear in my mind now, the voice of my now deceased, courageous Russian friend, Professor Taras Muranivsky, saying, "in the best way."

The "best way" signifies that the interest charges on the uttered funds must be decently low, probably in the range of 1-2% simple interest, and that the accumulation of added real (physical) capital exceeds the net Federal debt created in this way. This means, in turn, that we must concentrate the allotment of relevant Federal expenditures away from a "services economy," except as a temporary social measure of relief in the public interest, and, stay, absolutely, away from financial-speculative forms of investments, or, diversion of flows of national income into gambling, or, recreational drug use, or, kindred waste. The rate of increase of net physical output of the nation, must exceed the accumulation of the Federal debt.

This, of course, means a proportionately large commitment to increase of capital-intensity of investment in, in turn, the increase of physical productivity in the national economy as a whole. The needed balance of investment aims at a public sector of basic economic infrastructure outlays in the fairly estimated order of fifty percent, and requires an emphasis on scientific and technological progress, with emphasis on physical production and related investment. The increase of the physically defined productive powers of labor should be as measured in absolute, not percentile terms, and should express technological progress, rather than labor-intensity.

The development of the physical economy should be steered by the implications of a large-scale investment in nuclear fission as a power source, as a leading mode used in a massive program of desalination intended to cure illnesses of the physical economy such as reliance on fossil-water sources, and for the maintenance of other aquifers, the latter as typified by the case of the region from North Dakota down into West Texas. This must be accompanied by a vigorous commitment to bringing on the assortment of known and potentially knowable technologies associated with the large-scale, relatively early development of thermonuclear fusion, both as a power source for the economy, and for a crucial role in augmenting and otherwise managing so-called fossil resources.

The expansion of the space program should be seen essentially as a science-driver spearheading much of the applicable advances in technology needed for the improvement of the Earth-bound economy.

The FDR Paradigm

Such a program requires a return to the kind of thinking associated with a "fair trade," rather than "free trade" economy, and to thinking about physical and financial capital as we did under Franklin Roosevelt.

The principle on which the success of such a program depends, is the principle of fostering the increase of physical productivity, per capita and per square kilometer, through science-driven technological progress in the improvement of the productive powers of labor. This means technological progress as expressed by emphasis on a science-driver economy of the type which brought the U.S. and its allies to victory over Hitler et al. in the preparation for, and conduct of World War II.

Against the customary carping critics of such measures, consider the following.

Had Franklin Roosevelt lived, the freeing of the world from the imperial legacy of colonialism and the like, would have created a vast capital market for the products of a converted U.S. war production buildup, the reinvestment of the war debt margins in new capital formation, here and abroad, although it would have been associated with the combination of a temporary austerity, but a healthy accumulation of real capital. Our experience during the period of the Truman Administration, contained significant evidence in support of this benefit of a continued Rooseveltian, rather than a pro-colonialist Churchillian policy; but, under Truman's mistaken policies, the proportion of the benefit was just not enough.

The concept is clear, if we consider the facts of the matter from the standpoint of the principles of physical economy, rather than mere monetary theory. Indeed, it is monetarist thinking itself which is the source of the relevant great error in judgment on this subject.

Monetarist dogma assumes that the lending of money generates what monetarism regards as economic value. In fact, as the late John Kenneth Galbraith once said of the money lost in the 1929 crash and its aftermath: *it is only paper*. Under the U.S. Constitutional system, which is essentially a physical-economic system, rather than one premised on usury, the value associated with money is what a government is capable of making money do. As an example of this, consider the manner in which the U.S.A. must act now, to prevent what a deep collapse of the perceived value of the U.S. dollar would do, in triggering a chain-reaction of the entire world's economy into a virtual, or even actual "new dark age."

The New U.S. Dollar

Contrary to monetarist dogma, in reality, the value of the U.S. dollar since 1945 has been premised chiefly on the perception that the future value of the dollar is more or less fixed. So, at the close of World War II, the U.S. dollar was virtually the world's only stable currency, a dollar whose value was pegged to the assurance of a fixed-exchange-rate system tied, not to a gold standard, but to a far different proposition, a gold-reserve standard.

That system was undermined, chiefly by the combination of the effects of the ill-conceived U.S. war in Indo-China, and the wrecking of the physical economy of the United Kingdom under the first government of the Kingdom's Harold Wilson. The 1967-1968 succession of sterling and dollar crises intersected the effects of the Spring 1968 explosion of the 68ers, when 68er assaults against the "blue collar" strata, wrecked the influence of the Democratic Party's Kennedy legacy. Thus, the 1968 general election opened the gates for a stampede of wild-eyed monetarism throughout the 1970s. In the course of this stampede, the devaluation of the U.S. dollar, and the establishment of the floating-exchange-rate system, in 1971-1972, followed by the Rambouillet conference, created what was, in effect, an international monetary system based on an agreement to believe in the role of the U.S. dollar as the worldwide floating-exchange-rate system's own reserve currency.

The onrushing weakening, and threatened loss of belief in that worldwide U.S. dollar's role as an implicit reserve currency, threatens the rather immediate, chain-reaction-like collapse of an already rotted-out North American and European system; with the collapse of those sectors, the entire planet falls into a global new dark age. Meanwhile, the simmering state of the financial bubble built up on the base of expansion of the mortgage-based securities sectors in the U.S.A., Spain, and elsewhere, is one among the more important triggers for a general implosion of the world financial markets as a whole.

The potential for a monetary-financial and economic collapse of that sort will persist. However, the actuality of that threat can be controlled, if the perceived stable value of the U.S. dollar, over the medium to long term, can be maintained. It is not the monetary value of the dollar which is to be considered; but the political perception that the U.S.A., in concert with other partners, is committed to keeping that dollar at parity, functioning as a virtual world reserve currency, for purposes of scheduled settlement of accounts, over a generation or more to come. The nominal value of the U.S. dollar is therefore its political value, based on the reasonable confidence that accounts can be spread for settlement over the span of that forward period ahead.

The ability to make, and, even more delicate, to keep such promises, demands the erection of a system of protectionist agreements and measures among leading nations typifying the relevant regions of the world as a whole. State to state, and multi-state to multi-state agreements, especially long-term agreements, especially pro-protectionist agreements, would be the bulwark on which the prevention of a presently onrushing general collapse of the current system depends.

The protectionist agreements are needed for state-to-state relations; a sharp reversal of current "free trade" agreements, is also indispensable, for creating the conditions needed for building large-scale shifts from a so-called "service-economy" model, to a capital-intensive production model, within national economies. This form of protectionism does not imply a reduction in world trade; it requires a new physical-capital structure for an expanded, capital-intensive emphasis in technologically progressive, hard-commodity world trade.

Creating New Credit

The initial surge in any Federal program for economic recovery will be concentrated in investments in basic economic infrastructure, with emphasis on capital-intensive categories, such as power, especially nuclear-fission power, water management, mass transportation, rebuilding the infrastructure for technologically progressive family farming in what had been traditional agricultural regions, and reshaping urban regions. Drastic cuts in the cost to students of higher education will be required, and reorientation of primary and secondary education toward a science-technology, and Classical-culture-driven mode in classrooms of what had been traditionally moderate size a generation or two earlier.

The rebuilding of infrastructure, especially capital-intensive modes, will be the initial driver for reversing the preceding trend from an agro-industrial to a "services"-and-unemployment economy. The stimulation of recovery of private contract and related support for the installation of infrastructure, will move the process toward a resumption of the U.S.A.'s former mission as a leading agro-industrial economy of the world.

The general, longer-term perspective of recovery and development will be premised on the impact of very large-scale use of nuclear fission, plus an orientation toward the oncoming of thermonuclear-fusion-related technologies. These leading-edge technologies are essentially expressions of "high energy-density" effects in technology, and are, when employed in that mode, the upper end of productivity per capita and per square kilometer in the economy as a whole.

The current fad fairly described as the green-energy hoax, typifies the problem in thinking which must be corrected, if a collapse of the economy is to be avoided. Nuclear fission is presently the most efficient source of power. In certain modes, it is a source of local generation of hydrogen-based and related fuels from water, thus eliminating the reliance on the cost factor of transport of a low-grade material, better used as a chemical feedstock, petroleum, over long, and costly distances. The notion that corn could be the source of the nation's fuel for automobiles, is essentially a fraud, and deliberate hoax. The threat to the food supply from diverting agricultural areas to a gasohol or kindred program, is monstrous, especially if this is projected as currently forecast by relevant sources. The actual physical costs do not justify the claims, and the effect of relying on such sources of fuels would consume so much agricultural land, as to be the great granddaddy of all ecological catastrophes, for which some people's surviving families will live to curse the memories of the authors of such a murderous and inherently wasteful boondoggle forever.

What is probably the most interesting, and important aspect of the process of creating credit for productive investment on a large scale, is typified by the prospects for Eurasian development under the kinds of policies which I am projecting here.

Under our U.S. Constitutional system, credit is created through the lawful commitment of the Federal government to utter currency. The alternative, in world markets, is long-term treaty-agreements among nations. In the latter case, looking at prospects of cooperation among European and Asian nations, our attention should be chiefly focussed on bulk treaty-agreements with maturities of between a quarter- to half-century, agreements covering large-scale, long-term infrastructure investments, and production programs. Again, the recommended charge would be between 1-2% simple interest on primary, long-term credit.

Considering the size and condition of the population of Asia as such, much of the former industrial and related capacity of western and central Europe will be mobilized to meet the demand. As we see the portent in tendencies, on a more limited scale now, the overall program for Eurasia along such lines will tend to follow the streams from the capitals from Berlin to Moscow, to Beijing, and Delhi, as to other relevant capitals similarly. The U.S.A., while cooperating across the Atlantic and Pacific, will emphasize its partnership with revital-

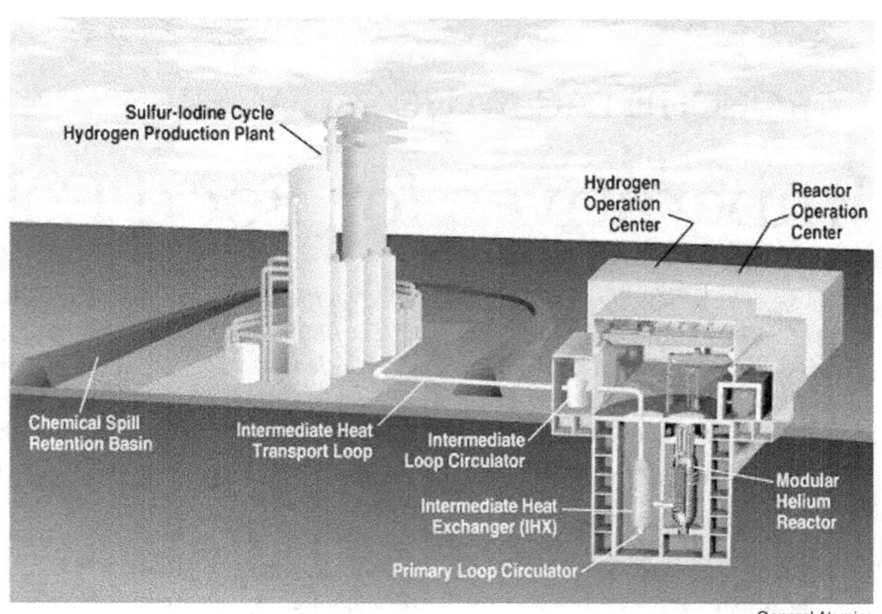

We need nuclear fission plants to provide local generation of hydrogen- based and related fuels from water. "The notion that corn could be the source of the nation's fuel for automobiles is essentially a fraud and a deliberate hoax." Here, a General Atomics design that couples a high- temperature helium reactor, the GT- MHR, to a sulfur-iodine cycle hydrogen production plant.

ized nations to our south. Together, we of Eurasia and the Americas will assume a leading responsibility for the rescue of Africa.

Without such perspectives, there is no immediate hope for an imperilled global civilization of today. For this mission, we require leaders who think in a certain way, who make and fulfill commitments in that certain way. Who does what is necessary to meet those goals, and who proceeds always, as what Friedrich Schiller identified as "world citizens and patriots," men and women who are true leaders, leaders who have subscribed to a mission for their nation, and also for all humanity? We must think of men and women who see the Creator's eye upon them in all that they do for the sake of the nations, and their people, as the situation requires. It is confidence and performance in the commitment to the mission, which will provide the popular confidence needed to bring the mission to success. In that way, we need not fear the great crisis now immediately before us. It is the restored confidence of peoples in their governments, a renewed confidence of the people in the meaning of the outcome of their own lives, which will, if we allow that, get us, get the world safely through the monstrous storm of crisis now closing in upon us, from all sides.

Imperatives for Food Policy

July 13—The following dialogue took place on the July 13 LaRouche PAC National Activists' Call. *Participating in this call were several of the speakers and other participants in the International Food for Peace Conference, "Food For Peace & Thought: China-U.S. Agricultural Cooperation," held in New York City on July 7.*

Dennis Speed: Last Friday there were two historic meetings. One was in Europe, the G-20 Summit, where despite all of the attempts to stop it from happening, President Donald Trump and Vladimir Putin of Russia actually met and had a discussion which was described by various commentators, including in the United States, as potentially one of the most important meetings since the War, and I think they meant the Second World War. Prof. Stephen Cohen, an important commentator in the United States, commented that perhaps what we have seen is Donald Trump emerge as a major American statesman as a result of that meeting.

The other thing that we should definitely point out is that last Saturday, simultaneous with the meeting of the G-20, the Schiller Institute, the Foundation for the Revival of Classical Culture, and China Energy Fund Committee, held a joint symposium at which 32 representatives of Chinese industry, as well as government and non-government organizations, participated in a forum with about 175 persons from the Schiller Institute and media that came to cover it. That conference, which took up specifically the issue of advanced agricultural capability to feed the world, actually took place as a way of allowing the United States—the process of the United States joining the Silk Road—a way to get into the highest levels of this actual discussion.

Helga Zepp-LaRouche prepared a video for that conference. What was important about what she emphasized, was that you can't take up any matter, whether it's agriculture or whether it's new infrastructure processes, or other elements—you can't pick up anything like this without looking at the core relations between Russia, China, and the United States. What we are seeing—what we are involved in right now—is obviously an attempt by treasonous factions both based in the United States and also factions around the world, for that matter, trying to destabilize the Presidency, even though that victory occurred on Friday.

You know, we call these "fireside chats," and on Saturday of last week, the conference or sections of the conference visited the FDR Presidential Library Museum and FDR's home. About 25 members of the Chinese delegation went there, and another 35 or so Schiller Institute and other members went. When you are at that location and you hear the discussion, and you

Jason Ross

Speakers on Panel I of the July 7 conference—"Food for Peace and Thought: U.S. China Agricultural Cooperation." Right to left: (former) Mayor DeWayne Hopkins, Muscatine, Iowa; Dr. Patrick Ho, Deputy Chairman, and Secretary General, China Energy Fund Committee, Hong Kong, China; Lan Huasheng, Chairman of the Board, Shenszhen Dasheng Agriculture Group; Wei Zhenglin, Agriculture Attache, Embassy of China; Robert L. Baker, Agriculture specialist, EIR, and Schiller Institute; Dr. Carl Pray, Professor and Chairman, Department of Agriculture, Food and Resource Economics, Rutgers University.

Shown here on the steps of the home of Franklin Delano Roosevelt is a 25-person Chinese delegation with 35 Schiller Institute members from Metro New York City, for a tour on July 8 of Hyde Park, including the FDR Library, and the Henry Wallace Center.

think about what Roosevelt did in the time of his Presidency, and you then put that in the context of what JFK did for the space program, when you look at what President Trump has been saying concerning issues of state and the fact of the meeting between himself and Vladimir Putin, and then the meeting with Xi Jinping—there is a clear basis for the country to be moved forward.

And it is to be moved forward from the highest platform of space technology—space technology applied to industry, to agriculture, and to the revolutionizing of the very machine-tool process, the process by which all forms of activity are done in the world.

At this point, I'm going let Ben Deniston take it. He spoke at our conference, and gave a conference presentation which was rooted in making sure that the persons in the room were aware of the pivotal role of Lyn [Lyndon LaRouche] in his discoveries of physical economy, and in the formulation that became known as the World Land-Bridge.

Ben Deniston: I think it's appropriate to reflect back on what I think is the principle underlying the conference and what we're looking at now. Helga Zepp-LaRouche launched a whole series of international confer-ences, in which she started calling for a new paradigm of global relations and a concept that dovetails very well with the policy of win-win cooperation being promoted by the President of China. I think we certainly have a unique role in promoting Lyndon LaRouche's absolutely unique and original contribution to this entire discussion, because as Helga has emphasized, as our organization has emphasized, and as Lyn has emphasized, we're not talking about just fixing some problems in the world or alleviating some bad conditions—we're talking about what it is going to require to move mankind to a new historical stage, to a new level of humanity.

Helga has often referenced the comparison of mankind pre-renaissance—as looking at European culture as a reference point—pre-renaissance human civilization as compared to post-renaissance human civilization. Mankind went through a qualitative, revolutionary change in what he actually represented as a creative species on this planet. That is something that mankind uniquely does, and must always continue to do, and that's what we should be making in the present period, that level of historic change. This idea of the United States in an alliance with China and Russia—that is no joke—that is a power bloc that can take the world, and the Solar system and beyond, in a completely new direction.

The Underlying Conceptions

One thing we should keep up front and at the center is what is the idea, what are the conceptions underlying that new direction? One thing that I highlighted in my speech, which I think is worth bringing up again, is that Helga has recommended ending geopolitics, and Mr. LaRouche's work provides an invaluable and necessary grounding for that, in getting rid of this idea of a "zero-sum game," or this "limits to growth" idea which really underlies a lot of the geopolitical thinking today.

This idea that we're all in a race to control some finite amount of wealth on this planet, and we're up against other nations, other cultures, and other peoples, in attempting to access and control what we can get before "they" can get to it, and to undermine the ability of other nations to get to these resources or these technologies before we do, and so on. We have entire discussions about how the British Empire has pioneered this bestial way of thinking. The point is, that is false, that is not only an inhuman way of thinking—suppressing the development of other nations.

The conference that we held was on the subject of food for peace. Food has been a major means of control by these types of forces. The British used controlled, induced famines with horrific results to control the population of India, for example. This is just one example of how this type of thinking has led to the geopolitical suppression of populations, the suppression of the development of people. That idea must end. It doesn't end by just saying, "Hey, that's bad, and we shouldn't do that to people." That's true, but there's a deeper issue, which Mr. LaRouche has defined very uniquely, in his work, which is that mankind is an absolutely unique force on this planet, that can by its very nature fundamentally revolutionize and change its relationship to the environment. There is no such thing as fixed resources available to mankind.

You can take any example. Some people are saying that water is the new oil, it's the new shortage in the coming generation or two; water is going to become a scarce resource that we're going to compete over, and financial interests are already trying to position themselves to take advantage of it. It's all crazy. If we develop the infrastructure system and new technologies needed—there's more than enough water on this planet to provide all of the agricultural, urban industrial needs, human needs, biospheric needs for a much greater population than we have today. This requires applying the technologies we have available.

You have craziness about control of energy supplies—people believe they are competing to control these finite supplies of coal, oil, natural gas, what have you—when we already know that it is just a pittance compared to the power supplies available to mankind with nuclear reactions—the energy reactions of nuclear power, fission and especially fusion. You just look up at our Moon; our Moon is covered in helium-3, probably the best fusion fuel we know of, which will provide not just fusion power, but the most advanced form of fusion power that has many additional benefits. We could supply a much larger population and higher living standards.

This is a very real, very historic, very exciting period we're in; again, I think we have a unique role as messengers of Lyndon LaRouche's underlying ideas—not just ideas, but the scientific principles on which this

The Chinese delegation and Midwest farmers sample milk at their July 8 visit to the Shenandoah Farm, in Duchess County, N.Y., which is part of a 10-farm cooperative marketing "Hudson Valley Fresh" products. See www.hudsonvalleyfresh.com

new paradigm is based. It can't just be a negation of bad things; it must be premised on a higher principle, a positive recognition of what it is that makes our species unique. We have different cultures, we have different nations, we have different histories, but we can come together around a unified principle of humanity, around shared growth and development based on that principle. That has to be the positive conception carrying us forward, and I think it was reflected very strongly at this event with this delegation from China, a very interesting delegation who got a chance to meet some American counterparts—in our organization there are representatives of farm leaders, of agriculture in the United States. I think that's just typical of the kind of dialogue and collaboration and coordination that we can be moving toward.

China's Achievements

Marcia Merry Baker: The conference on July 7 in Manhattan was followed on July 8 by a trip to Hyde Park, where Franklin Delano Roosevelt's home is, and a visit to a dairy farm operation that's typical of such farms outside big cities, so there was a lot of opportunity to talk. What came through in the presentations—about twelve of them in the day-long conference, six or seven from China and then some from the United States—what comes through is that in the last 40 years or more,

China has upgraded its agriculture deliberately to achieve a very secure food supply. The speakers from China described how they did it, and how they upgraded the diet that people have every day.

The principle behind it is that a population can go ahead and do that for its own nation, and we can collaborate between nations. But what that implies is the opposite of what we hear in the United States. We're told that it's the markets, not your government, that has to decide whether you

Wikimedia commons
Famine in colonial India in 1943 was met then, with inaction by the British. Food shortages, present day neo-British Empire defenders say, are inevitable.

are going to improve your agriculture or not, whether you're going to have enough to eat or not, and whether you will respond if there's an emergency like there is now overseas in Yemen, or South Sudan, or somewhere else that needs food. This was very outstanding.

In short, what several of the people from China described, is that by 1984 they had achieved enough grain production (wheat, rice, and other grains) to make China's food supply secure. No need to worry; they even had a surplus. So then, what did they do? They had maybe many hundreds of millions of people by then, eight hundred million or so.

They decided they could take some of the land out of food and put it into cotton, because "we need that." We can take some of the grain capacity we have for rice and wheat, and we'll produce corn for livestock or wheat for livestock, so they did that. And then, after another 20 or more years or even 30 years, instead of only 8% of their grain capacity going to feed meat animals (hogs, cattle, and chicken), now close to 30% of the grain they produce goes to these meat animals—and their diet was improved to have a lot more pork, a lot more eggs, and a

Library of Congress
Rural electrification, one of FDR's major initiatives, in California's San Joaquin Valley in 1938.

lot more dairy and milk.

This has been done deliberately, and the nature of what has been done has gone hand in hand with bringing 700 million people out of poverty over the same time period. This model is the kind of model that you can have for the world, and it isn't as if people didn't know how to do it—but we've been told in the last 40 years by the neo-British Empire types that we'll always have a food shortage—not true!

So the conference was very exciting. Remember, think for a minute, that twice in our own history, whatever age we are, we know about Abraham Lincoln, and that his government organized advances in agriculture. For example, there was the Homestead Act that gave away 160 acres out in Oklahoma if you would agree to farm and improve it—a deliberate intervention. Then fast forward to President Franklin Delano Roosevelt in the 1930s, during the Depression. Deliberate measures were taken to lift people out of poverty and put people to work, even in the rural areas through the Civil Conservation Corps. Also, FDR developed electricity in rural areas to reduce poverty.

I'm only pointing to those two interventions, because the United Nations right now is meeting on how to eliminate world poverty by 2030. It's called "Agenda 2030" or the "2030 Project." There has been talk like this for decades—how can we get people out of poverty? If you don't change the system, you will never do it. But now, we have the active mobilization by China in collaboration with Russia, and the offer to the United States to work with them is on the table. Agriculture people got together on this here, and said "now we can use the China model, which is really the American System model, and we can succeed." The goal is still there for 2030, and what we had on July 7 and 8, just with a dialogue, is for real. There are a lot more specifics that I could tell you about, but this much is illustrative.

Speed: Very good Marcia. Thanks a lot. I want to point out a couple things that we want people to do. What we're telling you about here is two things: One, there was a major victory when Trump actually did meet with Vladimir Putin. That has been seen, but everybody on these phone calls knows we've been talking about it for months as something that needed to happen. It was something that every major intelligence agency in the world (on the wrong side, that is) deployed against, and it happened nonetheless. Now, the next phase has to be to get Trump to act against Wall Street, but the way to do that is not by asking him. *The way you do it is, you've got to go out and do something.* We've had a lot of discussions about this over the past weeks. There is this silliness that supposedly the President is supposed to come in and change everything—and people applaud it. It doesn't work that way.

All a President is supposed to do actually, is to respond to the initiatives being taken by the American citizenry, and obviously he ought to have his own ideas, as well; but the American citizenry has the obligation to advocate and to organize for changes in policy and changes in the direction of the country. That is what we understand. That's not something that we happen to have an ambition to do; that's a responsibility of citizenship.

I see we have some questions, and also, I just want to say that if there are people who were at the conference, please get in the queue and let's see what we can do here.

Question: This is Alvin here in New York. My question is, we have Congress still in session, so should we not be looking to mobilize and organize our citizens not only for the petition drive, but to get down there to the Hill and begin the process of raising the roof on Glass-Steagall once again? They're still in session. We have some time. This is a national call. There are people here from everywhere, and I just wanted to raise that, so that we should start next week to organize and get some turnouts, not just a handful of people. My question is, can we do that and should we do that starting next week?

Speed: I know that the Senate is in session; I'm not sure about the House. I'll put it like this: Since people are on the call from around the country, one of the better things for them to be able to do, of course, is going to see people in their districts. That always has a tremendous impact, and two or three people going to see somebody in the districts is an excellent idea. With regard to the Senate, that's true. I suppose that we just ask about that and see what the viability of that is. That's my own answer. I don't know if Ben or Marcia has anything to say.

Urgent Messages from Farmers

Marcia Baker: I want to fill one thing in. A couple of the messages to the conference last week, from farm leaders in the Farm Belt (Kansas and Indiana), concerned exactly what you said, Alvin, about Glass-Steagall, and making a shift and ordering what must be done in the country. I'll read you just a couple of sentences from James Benham. He's the President of the Indiana Farmers Union, and he sent this in last Friday. He quoted what he said in 2013 when he sent out a public letter, which said, "We must return to economic policies which protect the nation's ability to produce. Glass-Steagall will cut the speculators off from the public trough, the first step to restoring a sound banking system and setting up a production-tied credit system." He went on to say, "pass Glass-Steagall and we can get on to the business of rebuilding our nation. Then we'll be able to pass farm and food-supply legislation based on the principle of decent parity pricing for farmers, and get food security for Americans and have domestic production and reserves."

Just as Dennis said, in different home districts, a huge impact can be made. Some people may be on the phone from the Farm Belt states to elaborate on this.

Question: Hello, this is J. from Iowa. I've lived my life in agriculture. I want to ask Marcia a question or two here: Marcia, you were commenting on China launching its agriculture infrastructure, if you will? Is that done by private citizens as I am, or is that done by government organization?

Merry Baker: Well, the exciting thing is, it's both, as I understand it. For one thing, there's a five-year plan, and over something like the last thirteen years, almost three five-year plans. Every year there's a January report on the state of agriculture by the government, so the government lays out both: "Here's what we'd like to see," and the government gives grants for such things as irrigation systems.

The government does send people into the poorest,

Chinese visitors speak with the owner of Shenandoah Farm, and family members, at their porch, July 8. The property has been in their family since 1892, now specializing in the milk herd, and in corn, alfalfa, and pasture.

most rural villages to do some work on helping figure out what can be done, like putting together a list of all four hundred families, and seeing what the land is like. But the individual decisions are still made by actual farmers on the land. I'm giving you some examples, because it's definitely a decision that's made from the top, through the government—but then, when it gets implemented, it's implemented on the ground by actual people. It isn't some kind of government-run plantation; it's not like the old British East India Company plantations as I understand them.

Follow-Up: Well, this is a huge concern of mine, and there should not be hungry people in any corner of this world, as far as I'm concerned. I know that I run a relatively small-scale farm compared to some, but I figured it up one time, off of USDA standards, and with what I produce in cattle and grain, I should be able to feed 950 to 1,050 people every day of the week, 365 days of the year.

And the problem that I have with everything that's going on, is, I borrowed three-quarters of a million dollars in January, hoping that the speculators would let me make at least that much by December, so that I could pay my bills. At the same time, you go to the grocery store and a lot of the people that I'm talking about feeding, can't afford to buy what I produce and put on those shelves. And that absolutely drives me nuts, because I risk my livelihood in losing everything for the fourth generation now, and we don't get rewarded—nor can people that are soon to be hungry—they can't afford

what we're producing. Somewhere in the middle, somebody's taking a huge cut: Marcia, what does a rib-eye steak cost where you come from?

Marcia Baker: I don't know! I have to ask someone else on the phone. [laughs]

Follow-Up: Because if it's over $2.75, you're getting charged a lot more than I'm getting for it.

Marcia Baker: Oh yeah, we're talking about $9.

Follow-Up: That's the difference, is what I'm saying. Also, we can only do what we are capable of out here, and then the rules and regulations on everything that we are doing are getting so stiff—I have to have a thirty-seven point check list to take care of pigs every day. Those kinds of things just seem absolutely crazy to me. I've been doing it for 30 years, and now some guy that has never raised a pig in his life tells me what checklist to make every day, to make sure I'm doing it the proper way.

So I guess, with what China's doing, the United States already has the highest regulations to make sure the food is as clean and as healthy as it can be. And I see countries like China—and I read some of the reports also, that say what China is doing and getting ready to do—we are already here, but not in a fashion that it is going to work, and we have farmers that are going broke every year doing the same thing that we can't get rewarded for …

I know that something has to change, and has to change relatively soon, but I guess the hard part here, is nothing happens on the timeline that I think it should. But you know, something's got to change here: There should be no hungry people in this world. And China is doing the absolutely right thing! They're going to make sure their people stay as full as they can, and I appreciate that.

Speed: Great! We have a lot of other people on the line. I'm going to go to the next one, but thank you very much for that. I think that was really helpful for people.

Question: Hello, this is D. in Florida. I come from a West Texas oilfield background; I'm taking an interest in greenhouses, as well as the economy and management set-up. So the call from the fellow in Iowa was very interesting to me, as he has an inside viewpoint that I'm not real well acquainted with ... Would the National Bank be able to help him out with his financing? And then would it go through a state bank, or would it be more like the IRS, where it bypasses the states and goes directly from the Federal to the individual?

Marcia Baker: Well, I think we have several things, but to keep it simple, and on principle, I think the point is that of course, farmers do need credit to operate, by season. They need it when they need it, for the planting, for the harvests, and for the other functions. So the point is, if you have sound banking, instead of this wild Wall Street bail-out banking system we have right now—if you have sound banking with community banks chartered properly, you would have, as we had before, loans for when farms, businesses, and genuinely useful functions and activities need it—not to mention credit for infrastructure projects—irrigation, water management, and transportation.

So that is what we need, and there would be no problem between the state and Federal level. We must put in the Glass-Steagall law, so that you have commercially useful banking as we've just described it, totally separate from any kind of speculative financial house. We understand that.

And in particular, we need a National Bank, a national institution that can be a primary coordinator for funds and investments, and including international investments. China has said they're willing, in fact, to put in the directed credit for the larger projects—the ones that we need for upgraded nuclear power systems, water systems, and waterway repair of locks and dams—a whole new level.

Back to the farmer, the problem that we've had is not just the repeal of Glass-Steagall banking in 1999. We also had, a year later, what's called the Commodities Futures Modernization Act, which allowed anything-goes speculation on the Chicago Mercantile Exchange, on and off exchanges. We can restore credit by government mandate, so that we can have sucessful individual farms. And we must also return to parity-based pricing to cover your costs of production.

And Dennis Speed described the trip last week to a farm outside New York City, which is a dairy farm. Milk is perishable; the dairy situation in the United States now is in complete crisis, because the prices don't cover production, and you've spent years developing your dairy herd—and you have to keep feeding those animals every day. So that's in a crisis. We've had three or four years of grain prices being under the cost of production. That doesn't have to be.

In fact, it's the system we have, and that's why we're seeking to force a change in the whole thing. It's so crazy that last year, the Obama government filed a lawsuit against China in the World Trade Organization, asserting that China was putting a floor under the prices for its corn growers. So the corn growers in China get a certain price. And the U.S. government suit said that should not be allowed, because it takes away the opportunity for American farmers to be able to produce and have a market. That's crazy! It's to the benefit of everyone, to have "win-win" agriculture, and for nations to decide what their farmers need, because that's the way everybody can eat.

That's the short answer.

A New Ice Age?

Follow-Up: I sure appreciate that. One other question that affects agriculture. What's the review on the possibility of a coming ice age? I look at spaceweather.com on the sunspot cycles, and we have had more sunspot-less days this year, already this year, than all of last year.

Deniston: Sure, that's absolutely true. There's a longer-term and shorter-term cycle, which we probably want to distinguish when people talk about an ice age. We tend to be talking about cycles on the order of tens of thousands to 100,000 years. So we're currently in what's called an Interglacial, a period in between two ice ages. Now a full-on ice age is when you have a mile-thick sheet of ice down to the area of Chicago, and it reaches all the way up north; those changes tend to be more on the tens of thousands to hundred thousand-year timescales.

But you're correct in noting that the Sun is getting weak. It's getting very weak, the weakest we've seen really since we have had modern instrumentation in the past couple of generations. There's strong evidence that the Sun is going into a period of low activity that we haven't seen in four hundred years. The last time this occurred—that we saw this very weak solar activity—it corresponded with what is called the "Little Ice Age," which is different from the larger ice ages. It was a period of prolonged, dramatic cooling that affected the planet in the 1600s. That is definitely something that we need to be thinking about.

Climate does change. It changes by natural variation, and we should be thinking about how mankind can come to control those processes, and ensure that we can

Eli Santiago

Members of the Jackson family (with hats) answer questions from their visitors. They described the pressures on their farm from urbanization, taxes, and soaring insurance costs, while dairy prices to the farmer—nationwide—are too low. Family members work off the farm as well. One Canada-based visitor was surprised to find there is not a pricing and production policy for U.S. dairy farmers, like that in Canada.

maintain agriculture, the viability of the biosphere, and human economic activity in the context of the climate changes which are going to occur. So those are the kinds of things we should be thinking about, and thinking about how we should prepare ourselves. How do we actually begin to control some of these processes and influence these things? That's something that's not really that far away at this point, if we decide to come together to do that.

Follow-Up: That sounds good to me. I sure appreciate your explaining it.

Speed: Is Bob Baker here? Bob spoke at our conference. He gave a terrific presentation about the application of space technology to agriculture. And as you go into that, Bob, I think the story that Ron Wieczorek told us about his brother, and how much land he farmed, and what his situation is, I think that might be relevant for people to hear, because it's so apparently unbelievable.

Bob Baker: Well, the situation is—and Ron may be on the phone. Ron's father raised six kids on a 300-acre farm and did quite well, but today, there are known cases where people have 50 thousand acres and a half-billion-dollar investment or more, and they've lost money for the last three years. And when we discussed this with the Chinese delegation over the weekend, they

were completely awestruck. They couldn't imagine that that would be possible.

And that doesn't mean that the farm isn't productive, and it doesn't mean that the people aren't highly skilled—they are very skilled. They do precision agriculture with the highest-tech machinery, but the marketplace just doesn't have the price structure necessary to keep smaller farmers in business. And thus, we've seen a steady evolution, where the marginal farmers keep falling backwards, and then bigger farms develop, because they're farming on smaller and smaller margins, and *very* deep in debt.

That is not the American System. It's not the system Alexander Hamilton had in mind, or the other Founding Fathers, and it's not the way the nation ran even back in Franklin Roosevelt's period. Because Roosevelt actually found the policies that you might say we're on right now when he came into office—a massive crisis in agriculture, farms driven into bankruptcy everywhere, unavailability of credit, and prices down. But just by executive order, Franklin Roosevelt said, "there'll be no more farm foreclosures." He outlawed all farm foreclosures, and he set up a national credit system—and within one year they refinanced all the farmers that were in trouble in the United States. And that's just indicative of the magnitude and the power of government of the American System, if it's determined to do that.

Now, I just might add a couple of things, because a lot of people even in agriculture don't understand—or maybe aren't one hundred percent aware of—the consolidation of our food production into the hands of a very few people. We have 2.2 million farmers in the United States, but only 10% of those farmers produce 75% of the food. That means 90% of U.S. farmers produce the other 25%. Most of them are subsidizing that food production with one or two non-farm jobs. Also, if you look at the consolidation of many parts of the food industry,— Take the pork industry. The United States is the world's third-largest producer and largest exporter of pork. And

90% of U.S. pork is produced by 1% of the U.S. farmers! That's a shocking figure if you think about it.

If you look at chickens, the United States is the world's largest chicken producer, the largest exporter, but 95% of all the chickens in the United States are produced by 1% of the U.S. farmers.

Dairy: The world's largest producer and exporter of cow's milk, but *twenty* giant dairy entities produce 76% of all the milk in the United States. That's a vertically integrated operation.

And I could go on. The beef industry—5% of the feedlots in America produce 85% of all the beef. And so we could go on and on. The United States is the biggest producer of ethanol in the world, the biggest exporter of ethanol, and the biggest *importer* of ethanol! And we import it from Brazil, which is the second largest producer of ethanol, and its biggest export market is the United States, and our biggest export market is to Brazil! That's pretty amazing.

Those parameters give people some sense of the magnitude of the monopolization of food production in America, to say nothing of the grocery stores, which all are continuing to merge, because they can't make it.

Speed: Thanks a lot, Bob, that was very useful, and I think will shock the hell out of people.

We've been saying—if you're doing things, we have a lot of people who go out and deploy in the street, and we invite people to do that if you're in touch with your regional office— that's important. But getting out there to actually advocate the Four Laws: Glass-Steagall; a national bank; and a new credit system with directed credit for purposes of our industry, and agriculture, and infrastructure; and then, of course, energy.

One thing that Ben Deniston pointed out, is the issue of energy density. What we were talking about at the conference, and what we introduced to the Chinese delegation, was Lyndon LaRouche's idea of energy-flux density. The notion that you've got to somehow fight the whole world for scarce resources, is not true. It falls on its face when you take technological progress into account, and you use the idea, for example, of thermonuclear fusion.

Forty years ago it was calculated that one cubic mile, I believe it was, of the Earth's crust, using fusion technologies, could provide the raw materials for all the industries in the world for a year—and that was back in the 1970s that that was calculated. And therefore, when people give these arguments about how thermonuclear fusion is forty years in the future, the thing they have not considered is, what if there had been a full-scale crash program for thermonuclear fusion in the 1970s? What would have been the significance of that for ending dependence on oil or natural gas as fuel sources, and also, what would have been the significance in terms of the efficiency of production?—of energy production as well as industrial production for the world as a whole?

So the British-intelligence, new colonialist view of the necessity for scavenging and somehow killing other people, or cannibalizing the world because of our needs—that is something we should *never, never* give in to. And if you go out and deploy with us, that's an idea we can definitely overcome.

What Our Farmers Need Now

Question: This is Ron Wieczorek from South Dakota. I was at the conference, and I would just like to thank everybody that had something to do with making that conference happen. I was sad that I could not see a thousand farmers there, but I understand the reason why, when we look at the total number of farmers. Bob was talking about 2.4 million farmers. I believe it was back in the 1930s and the 1940s, there were 33 million farmers! They had political clout. Ben, the Farmers Union man that you were referring to, made a comment about 220,000 Farmers Union members. In the 1930s and the 1940s, there were 10 million members, when the total population was half of what it is today.

So the percentage of farmers was high; we had real political clout because of the numbers. Our farmers today have to merge, and the farmers that are out there are going to have to organize for outreach, so we can increase the number; we can't increase the number with the farmers—we have to create the numbers that support Lyn's Four Laws, and without Lyn's Four Laws this country is not going to make it.

I mean, we've got to have Glass-Steagall on the books, and we've got to have a New Bretton Woods system that gives a parity ratio to the currencies of the world so you can have just trade, rather than having speculators running the currency values up and down. We have to have a parity pricing! My grandson asked me this afternoon, why we don't have a world price for food? I believe the Chinese and the Japanese are getting something like $9 or $10 for their corn, and that's three times what we're getting for our corn; of course, it costs a lot of money to ship our corn there, but somebody's still making a lot of money on the movement of this

(Former) Mayor DeWayne Hopkins, of Muscatine, Iowa, speaks with a member of the Chinese delegation, on their visit to the Hudson Valley dairy farm July 8. Hopkins fielded many questions about Iowa farming, and what Chinese President Xi Jinping has done on his two visits to Muscatine—now a sister city to Zhengding, China.

corn around the world.

Those are just some of the things I wanted to comment on.

Speed: I have a question for you, Ron. Didn't you do a meeting in the last couple of days, when you got back?

Follow-Up: Yesterday morning I started calling people, I don't know how many calls I made, but it was a number, and last night we had a meeting with twelve people who showed up. One state legislator called and wanted to meet with me later, because he had a prior commitment. I had four other people say they had prior commitments, too. So I think people are really interested in what's going on, especially in our area out there. Many of the people that attended were farmers, but not all—at least half were working people.

But in South Dakota here, our land prices have been run up by some speculators. We've had a 365% increase in our land values since 2009. And a lot of these farmers are "rich" by their assets. And this has nullified a lot of

the suffering on the farm, especially of the older farmers, because they feel comfortable with this high-priced land they got. But that can't last, and when that starts crumbling, the banking factions are very worried about this farm crisis, or food crisis, or whatever you want to call it.

I just a spoke with a banker who has a bank in Iowa. There was a farmer in Iowa who two years ago lost $6 million, and last year, he lost another $10 million. Now the only reason he could still operate, is because of inflation on his land. It's not because of anything that he got paid for; it's just that the assets that he had have tripled in value, or even more than that. So he still has financial statements that show assets—and I don't know how long that can go on. I think if we remember 1984, when they cut land values in half here in South Dakota, and the farmers' machinery values in half—it was a devastating time, and we lost a hell of a lot of farmers to suicide.

Speed: You just brought up something that I want to make sure *everybody* understands: *Now* you people should understand that Glass-Steagall is literally a matter of life and death. Because if you don't have food, if your country doesn't have farmers,— you heard Bob Baker's evaluation earlier about pork, and about the percentage of food being grown by so few people. I think what is important for us all to get, is the fact that you listened to the conference on Saturday, Ron, and you traveled on Sunday. Now it's Thursday. You had a meeting on Wednesday. So that means that you got back and basically organized the thing in three days.

I want this to be clear to everybody on the phones, because we have about 30, 31 states or so on every phone call. If we were doing that, and begin doing that—and again, let's look at Glass-Steagall, because it's the one thing that we can all see now, whether we're talking about food, or we're talking about housing, about individual employment, or industry. It's clear that this is a means, not merely for Glass-Steagall, but this idea of a new credit system and the Four Laws as you said, Ron. That is where we've got to strike.

The deployments are one part; the meetings are another part; this phone call is another way that people can be activated, as we're seeing from this experience tonight. So I just want to interject that. We're going to move on, Ron, but that report was invaluable, and in the aftermath of the conference, we should make sure that this is an element that we keep in the consciousness of all the people that are coming onto our phones. Thanks a lot.

Question: Hi, this is Andy Olson from Minnesota. I was at the conference, but I got on the call late tonight, so I don't know exactly what transpired, but here's just a little bit of an idea of what I got out of the conference. It was American farmers there, plus the Chinese, who represented a big part of their agriculture. So theirs is a command economy, which is working well for them, and ours is supposedly the American System, we're the independent farmer—but I really believe the American System is being watered down. And it's really alarming when you see that farmers have been moved into this idea of contract farming—they contract essentially with an entity that deals with the cartels. And it's happened in meat especially—in pork, broilers [chicken], milk, and beef. And in crops not so much, but that's starting to occur also.

And we have to realize what is happening to us— and I don't think that even I have been aware of how far this has gone. I don't know how to stop it, but I think dialoguing with the Chinese was really useful. They can see what we are faced with, or maybe got an inkling of what we're faced with, and were surprised that we were under this kind of attack. And we could see what success they are having, and it's pretty impressive. So it's the beginning of a dialogue that I think will be positive in the future.

Speed: That was great, because you summarized for a lot for people who were not there, not only your own response to what happened, but actually—that was precisely what it was for. It was a promissory note for a more in-depth discussion that now needs to be engaged in. So I want to thank you for saying that.

I think we'll go to closing responses, Marcia, from you and then from Ben.

Marcia Baker: One thing we're going to do at the request of our South Dakota friend, Ron, is have a press release on the follow-on, not just to the event on Friday, but also looking to what we need to do, here and now, right now, in this country. We will emphasize the Four Laws, and emphasize the discussion that's gone on between the very high-level Chinese delegation, and our farm-based representation from South Dakota, Minnesota, and Iowa. We also had messages from Kansas and Indiana. And Dennis, I'm going to do that press release in the next couple of days for Ron and other people in the Midwest.

But this is our moment! With all the rotten stuff that we see being slammed against the institution of our Presidency, nevertheless there's tremendous opportunity.

Speed: Ben, would you like to summarize?

Deniston: Yes, only to say that we should take this as a call to go out and organize, and for each of us to go out and get more people on the call next week; we have our LaRouche PAC website—Dennis mentioned our report on the United States joining the New Silk Road, and the one on the Silk Road becoming the World Land-Bridge, that are available on our website in digital format. We have a lot of informational material there, and a lot of information that people need to organize around these ideas. We have all this available, and we need to think about building our movement and building our impact, day to day, week to week, at this incredibly important time.

Coming out of this conference, with what's being discussed, it's exciting to hear how the entire nation can be mobilized and awakened in this way. You know, all this talk about the so-called "flyover states" across America that have been largely ignored by both parties—these are the people that have been building things—the last bastions of productivity, and they've been largely ignored. These are the people we need to mobilize now, to ensure that we can support Trump and push Trump to go with these programs, and everything outlined here.

Speed: The key idea is that there was a victory last Friday—Trump and Putin met. Trump and Xi met again. Xi and Putin have the best relations between China and Russia in history. This means, given what Lyn did for us, in his design of the Four Laws, the ball's in our court. We have a President who will respond if pushed. Our job is to push, and not just for what he is going to do, but to push our fellow citizens for what they are going to do.

I want to thank everybody for being on the phone call tonight. We have a Monday night call, for those who are doing organizing and want to get into the particular reports and nuts and bolts. Let's get more people on the call for next week.

Schiller Institute Addresses Serbia-China Conference in Belgrade

July 16—On July 12-13, the conference "Initiatives of the New Silk Road—Achievements and Challenges" took place in Belgrade, organized by the Institute of International Politics and Economics (IIPE) in Belgrade and the Institute of European Studies of the Chinese Academy of Social Sciences (CASS). Both institutes signed an agreement making the IIPE the Regional Center for Managing Scientific Projects as part of the cooperation format of the "16+1"—the 16 Central and Eastern European countries (CEEC) and China. Throughout the conference, the Serbian hosts and speakers prominently acknowledged the work of the Schiller Institute and of Helga Zepp-LaRouche personally, for advocating the New Silk Road policy.

EIRNS

Elke Fimmen (second from right), speaking at the July 12-13 conference in Belgrade.

The proceedings were opened by Branislav Dordevic, Director of the IIPE, followed by Serbian Secretary of State at the Ministry of Education, Science, and Technological Development Vladimir Popovic; the President of the Committee on Foreign Affairs of the National Assembly Zarko Obradovic; Li Manchang, Chinese Ambassador in Serbia, and by Mr. Huang Ping, Director General of the Institute of European Studies of CASS, who is also the Secretary General of 16+1 (CEEC) Think Tank networks.

Ambassador Li emphasized in his opening remarks that most of the projects in the context of 16+1 format have so far been implemented in Serbia. The first Chinese bridge in Europe was built here, the first visa-free arrangement between the two nations implemented, and the first steel mill in Europe bought by China. The first high-speed train project between Belgrade and Budapest will commence construction in November, as will other important industrial projects. He described the Belt and Road Initiative (BRI) as a house put up by China; but the entire interior design depends on input by its participants.

Last June, during President Xi Jinping's 2016 visit to Serbia, the just-concluded July 12-13 conference on the Danube River and the New Silk Road was jointly organized by the two institutes. This year, close to 50 scholars spoke at the one-and-half-day conference, representing 10 countries. Eleven speakers were from China (from CASS, the Chongqing Academy of Social Sciences, and from the Energy Development Research Center). It became clear that China has begun a more thorough approach to individual CEE countries, tasking teams of researchers to better understand the national characteristics of their partners.

Several of the Chinese speakers did not mince words on the problems faced by the Belt and Road Initiative policy in Europe, such as the EU's "protectionism," the anti-Russian sanctions, Ukraine crisis, and refugee problem, which will have to be solved, soon. Prof. Zhao Chen, chief of studies of international relations at the Institute of European Studies of CASS, dealt with BRI-European integration in his speech during the first session, "New Silk Road—Chinese Strategy of World Development."

Prof. Zhao drew attention to EU concerns about Chinese engagement in Europe, in particular the problem of investments by Chinese state-owned enterprises in Europe. Focussing on the positive cooperation between the EU and the BRI process, he noted that improvement of economic development in infrastructure increases local productivity. Therefore, he concluded, Western European countries should enjoy the spill-over effects, as they will be able to increase trade with such better developed new markets themselves. Since competition is not always bad, it could lead to better results and thereby force the EU to reform some of its outdated regulations and its bureaucratic system, which is itself protectionist.

In addition, he emphasized, the economic benefits of investment can prevent radicalization. The Belt and Road Initiative offers stability, which is important in regard to the problem of terrorism. He concluded, that it is not going to be an easy process, but this is a path of new possibilities in an uncertain era.

Elke Fimmen, representing the German Schiller Institute and *EIR*, spoke at the beginning of the first session on "The New Silk Road—Its Strategic Importance for World Peace." She was introduced by Prof. Duzsko Dimitrijevic, a professorial fellow of the IIPE and the main organizer of the conference, who announced that she was from "the famous institute from Germany." (In his concluding remarks for the day, Prof. Dimitrijevic again singled out the Schiller Institute's work and contribution.)

Elke Fimmen highlighted Helga Zepp-LaRouche's characterization of the Belt and Road Forum in Beijing, in which she participated, as a "very harmonious event," giving hope to the participants especially from developing countries, and that the Belt and Road policy exemplifies a new global paradigm of win-win-cooperation instead of geopolitics for the first time in history. Throughout Fimmen's 10-minute speech, the newly created German World Land-Bridge map was shown on the screen, drawing a lot of attention from the audience.

She focussed on the intensive diplomatic follow-up after the Belt and Road Forum summit, consolidating and expanding this spirit of cooperation for the benefit of world peace, leading up to the just-concluded G-20 Summit in Hamburg. Several noteworthy developments took place on the sidelines of the summit: the break-through meeting between Putin and Trump, and the cooperation between Trump and Xi—the Shanghai Cooperation Organization (SCO), as well as BRICS meetings, BRICS, Japanese-Russian-Chinese diplomacy, and above all the unprecedented new level of strategic cooperation between Russia and China on all levels.

If the leaders of China, Russia, and the United States can cooperate, she said, there is a chance to build a new global paradigm for peace and development, and to jointly overcome problems like underdevelopment, hunger, refugees, and the immediate danger of a financial crash.

One of the next speakers, Prof. Blagoje Babic, professorial fellow of the Committee for Economic Science of the Serbian Academy of Sciences and Arts spoke on "The New Silk Road—Response for the Challenges of the Chinese Economy." He closed his presentation with a moving personal reference to his pride in knowing for more than 26 years of the fight of Mrs. LaRouche and the Schiller Institute for the concept of a New Silk Road, which "incidentally" turns out to be the same concept that is now being realized by China.

The many interesting topics by Serbian, as well as speakers from Bosnia, Poland, Bulgaria, Romania, Russia, the United States, Germany, and of course China, will soon be published in a book by the IIPE.

Some of the highlights included a thorough review by Dr. Jasminka Simic, researcher and editor at RTS Serbia (National TV), on inter-regional connectivity and China's emphasis on setting the pace with future technologies and breakthroughs; and independent German space journalist Jacquelin Myrrhe—who had addressed the recent Krafft Ehricke conference in Munich—who emphasized that China's Space Program and the "Space Silk Road" supported global progress, which surprised the audience and had an uplifting effect. Edita Stojic Karanovic of the International Scientific Forum "Danube—River of Cooperation," spoke on the "New Silk Road and the Regional Cooperation of the Western Balkans" and the Morava-Vardar-Axios canal project.

A question was raised, as an interesting principled reflection, during the debate on the second day of the conference, about the "profitability" of Silk Road train connections to Europe. Dr. Jedrzej Czerep from the Amicus Europae Foundation in Warsaw pointed out that while at first, trains were going back to China empty, now better export-opportunities have led to a rise of local production in several sectors (mineral water, fruits, dairy products) and a higher volume of cargo shipped from Poland to China.

While there are obviously still many problems to overcome, not the least being the EU obstruction policies which have greatly contributed to the deindustrialization of Serbia, the overall process of discussion at this conference clearly showed the great potential for win-win cooperation between the Chinese Belt and Road Initiative, Serbia, and the other CEE countries and Europe as a whole.

But it is Western European countries—above all Germany—which have to change their approach quickly to a constructive one, instead of empty words and doctrinaire conditionalities—to not miss the boat of the paradigm change already taking place in this region of the world.

Putin-Trump Summit Yields Syria Progress; War Party Escalates Against Trump!

by Harley Schlanger

July 14—In an action which demonstrated true leadership and courage, U.S. President Donald Trump met with Russian President Vladimir Putin for more than two hours on July 7, during the G-20 summit in Hamburg, Germany. While the two addressed a broad range of strategic issues facing the two great powers, perhaps the most important immediate result was an agreement to jointly enforce a ceasefire in an area of southwestern Syria, as a step towards ending that horrific civil war, and defeating the Al-Qaeda/Al-Nusra and ISIS jihadist forces, which have inflicted such suffering on the Syrian people.

U.S. Secretary of State Rex Tillerson said this agreement demonstrates that the United States and Russia can collaborate: "This is our first indication of the United States and Russia being able to work together in Syria." Putin and Trump, he said, had a "lengthy discussion of other areas in Syria where we can work together." Tillerson commented on the "positive chemistry" which developed between the two, as key to the progress made.

This view was seconded by White House National Security Adviser H.R. McMaster, who said the creation of these "de-escalation zones" is a U.S. priority, "and we're encouraged by the progress made to reach this agreement." He added, "The United States remains committed to defeating ISIS, helping to end the conflict in Syria, reducing suffering, and enabling people to return to their homes. This agreement is an important step toward these common goals."

President Trump's initial reaction to this development was to tweet out, "Syrian ceasefire seems to be holding, Many lives can be saved. Came out of meeting [with Putin]. Good!" This view was shared by the UN Deputy Special Envoy for Syria, Ramzy Ezzeldin Ramzy, who described this as "a positive development."

Six days later, the ceasefire continues, with Russian military police coordinating efforts with U.S. and Jordanian military forces around the de-escalation zone. A joint Russian-U.S.-Jordan monitoring station is now operational in Amman, Jordan. As this is occurring, momentum is building to expel ISIS from Raqqa, its remaining stronghold in Syria, following their defeat at the hands of Iraqi forces in Mosul.

Since a military victory alone is not enough—given the damage done to the cities, villages, and infrastructure in Syria—it was highly significant that Imad Mustafa, Syrian Ambassador to China, met with Chinese officials in Beijing on July 9 to discuss what role China could play in reconstructing Syria. A delegation of Chinese business leaders will visit Syria in mid-August, to discuss projects in Damascus, Aleppo and Homs. Among them will be executives of the state-owned China Energy Engineering Corporation, and several major construction and engineering firms. Among the projects under consideration is building a Chinese-Syrian industrial park for 150 companies, which would create 40,000 jobs.

War Party Reacts

Instead of celebrating this progress, or at least grudgingly acknowledging some benefit from the

Trump-Putin summit, the anti-Trump/anti-Putin imperial war party has launched a frenzied escalation to either remove Trump from office, or cripple his efforts to break the United States out of the old geoplitical, unipolar world order which shaped the policies of Presidents Bush and Obama.

Donald Trump campaigned against this world order, attacking Hillary Clinton's support for Bush's Iraq War, and the regime-change wars in Libya and Syria. He warned that Obama's provocations against Russia and China risked the possiblity of a World War, saying that he believed it possible to collaborate with both Russia and China on matters of common interest, such as fighting terrorism, and increasing mutually beneficial trade and investment. Trump was clear on his commitment to reversing U.S. policy: "Cooperation with Russia is a good thing," he said, "not a bad thing; we both have huge nuclear arsenals; we can fight terrorism, we can end the constant wars."

Trump was elected because voters agreed that the endless wars were not successful in preventing terrorism—in fact, Bush's Iraq war, and Obama's commitment to regime change in Libya and Syria, increased the danger of terrorism, while piling up debt, and providing the excuse to expand the powers of the "surveillance state" against the American people. There was a war-weariness in the United States, which Trump recognized. Since shortly after the attack on the United States by British-Saudi terrorists on 9/11/2001, the United States has been at war. Every day during the Obama presidency, America was in a war. Had Hillary Clinton been elected, there likely would already have been tragic consequences by now, by mid-July or earlier, as from her stated commitments to challenge the Russians in Syria, and the Chinese in the South China Sea.

Make no mistake about this: Those now attacking the Trump-Putin summit are the ones responsible for the death and destruction in the war-zones throughout the world. As Schiller Institute founder Helga Zepp-LaRouche has been emphasizing, all the persistent and ugly noise about "Russiagate" has nothing to do with Russian "meddling" in the U.S. election, but is a reaction against the prospect that strategic collaboration between the United States, Russia and China—as favored by Trump—represents the end of the era of imperial wars and looting, based on dividing nations between East and West, and North and South—done on behalf of a collapsing financial system. The New Paradigm of peaceful cooperation and development which is emerg-

Official White House Photo by Lawrence Jackson

President Barack Obama, with Secretary of State Hillary Rodham Clinton, delivers a statement in the Rose Garden of the White House, Sept. 12, 2012, regarding the attack on the U.S. consulate in Benghazi, Libya.

ing and becoming unstoppable, will not be allowed—if they can possibly prevent it—by the merchants of death whose tight control over world affairs for the last decades is slipping from their grasp.

With Trump's victory, the "globalist" neo-cons who ran both the Bush and Obama Administrations, moved to prevent this challenge to their control over policy. The narrative of "Russian meddling," fed by networks in British intelligence, became the weapon they wielded against Trump. This story, concocted by British GCHQ and MI6 officials, was then spun by Bush-Obama networks in the intelligence community, spearheaded by former FBI Director James Comey, former CIA Director John Brennan, and Director of National Intelligence James Clapper—and it has dominated Trump's presidency from Day One.

The Democratic Party, reeling from the defeat of Hillary Clinton, has also mindlessly latched onto this, joined by Republicans such as Senators John McCain and Lindsey Graham. As we have documented, there has been no evidence to prove these claims, only "anonymous" source reports and leaks from intelligence officials, featured by mainstream media outlets determined to bring down Trump. Yet the story continues to evolve, with the latest chapter being what appears to be a sting operation, to entrap Donald Trump, Jr. into meeting with an alleged Russian official, Natalia Veselnitskaya, with dirt on Hillary Clinton—naturally, initiated by a British tabloid journalist, with Russian "connections"! While some are proclaiming this to be the elusive "smoking gun," it is unlikely to go anywhere, because, like the "dodgy dossier" of Trump's alleged sexual escapades in Moscow, it is too preposterous to gain traction.

However, as a result of this ubiquitous narrative that the Russians were responsible for Trump's victory, that Putin "owns" Trump, and that Trump has been "obstructing justice" to cover for his crimes, the meeting between Putin and Trump, which should have taken place shortly after Trump's inauguration on January 20 of this year, was put on hold. It is to Trump's credit, that in spite of the vicious and dirty operations against him, he proceeded with the summit in Hamburg anyway.

Courtesy Senate Select Committee on Intelligence

Director of National Intelligence James Clapper (center) testifies on worldwide threats to the U.S., before the Senate Select Committee on Intelligence Feb. 9, 2016. Clapper was accompanied by FBI Director James Comey (left), CIA Director John Brennan (right) and other top intelligence and security officials.

Freakout over the Summit

The breaking by the *New York Times* of the Trump, Jr.-Veselnitskaya story, which coincided with the Trump-Putin summit, is a transparent effort to derail the results of their meeting. But it is the sheer volume of hysterical attacks on Trump and Putin which demonstrates the hightened delusional state of the collapsing establishment.

Former CIA Director John Brennan, for example, one of the architects of Obama's support for anti-Assad jihadists in Syria, expressed open contempt for President Trump in a July 9 interview on NBC's "Meet the Press." Brennan said that Trump "ceded" ground to Putin by meeting with him, and by constantly raising "questions about the integrity and capabilities of the U.S. intelligence community." Brennan, who has stated that the Russians are permanent adversaries, took offense at Trump's statement that it was "an honor" to meet Putin, whom Brennan called "the individual who carried out the assault on our election. To me, it's a dishonorable thing to say."

Among Republicans, the anti-Trump tag team of Senators McCain and Graham, as usual, led the way. McCain scornfully characterized Trump's effort to work with Putin on cyber-security as absurd, and sneered that he's sure Putin could be of assistance in Trump's effort to prevent election hacking, "since he's doing the hacking." Graham accused Trump of having a "blind spot" when it comes to Russia, and added that not punishing Russia for interfering in the election "is undercutting his presidency."

The Democrats are even worse! While Senate Mi-nority Leader Chuck Schumer smeared the summit as "disgraceful," Hillary Clinton running mate in 2016, Virginia Senator Tim Kaine, went completely unhinged. "We are now beyond obstruction of justice," he sputtered. "This is moving into perjury, false statements, and even potentially treason." Many Republicans and Democrats echo Schumer's nonsense that there is no doubt that the Russians "deliberately interfered in our elections and sought to undermine and destabilize our democracy." As Schumer put it, Trump "seemed to acquiesce to Putin's denial" of Russian involvement, "almost certainly paving the way for future Russian interference in our elections."

On July 12, Rep. Brad Sherman, a California Democrat, became the first to introduce articles of impeachment against Trump, arguing Trump's alleged "obstruction of justice" in the case of former national security adviser Michael Flynn is enough to lead to his removal.

To combat this dangerous idiocy, which threatens not only to derail a serious potential for peace in the Middle East, but also an emergence of a New Paradigm of peace, based on realizing economic justice, Trump must continue to move in collaboration with Presidents Putin and China's Xi Jinping. A new era of mankind is on the horizon, as Helga Zepp LaRouche has been emphasizing. The promise of a victory over the terrorists and their British-U.S.-NATO supporters is within reach, as the first step to a global Renaissance. For this to be realized, Trump must join with the LaRouche movement in mobilizing the people of the United States into full support of this effort.

New, Worse Banking Crisis By the End of the Year?

July 13—Marco Zanni, an independent Member of the European Parliament from Italy, was interviewed yesterday on the anti-establishment, U.S.-based website, *Rogue Money*, by site founder "V, the Guerrilla Economist," along with *EIR*'s Harley Schlanger. Zanni focused on two points: the overall weakness of the EU banks and economy, which requires bank reform, beginning with Glass-Steagall, and the significance of U.S. President Trump's G-20 summit with Russia's President Vladimir Putin.

On the EU and the euro, Zanni reviewed the collapsing economy of Italy to highlight the overall problem. He said it is false to speak of economic recovery in the Eurozone—you cannot trust the statements coming from the European Commission (EC) or the European Central Bank (ECB). While the ECB pumping of liquidity may have temporarily saved some big banks from failure, it did so at the expense of the real economy, while doing nothing to address the systemic problems of Europe's Too-Big-to-Fail banks.

In Italy and Spain, the real rate of unemployment is over 20%, and real income is at 1999 levels. The recent bail-out/bail-in of two Venetian banks and the Monte dei Paschi bank showed the fraudulent nature of ECB policy, highlighting the reality that many banks are carrying unsupportable levels of debt, in the form of nonperforming loans and derivative obligations. There is growing anger in the population against the EC and the ECB, as well as against the Italian government for submitting to them.

Zanni said there are moves in the European Parliament, and especially in the Italian Parliament, to enact a banking reform policy, which includes Glass-Steagall banking separation, which his group is supporting. If this does not happen, he forecasts a new, more serious banking crisis by the end of this year or in early 2018, saying that this might lead to an Italian exit from the euro.

EDITORIAL

Asked about his view of the Putin-Trump summit, Zanni said he has been watching Trump "with great interest."

He has a "very positive view" of the Trump-Putin meeting. "Not all of Europe is against Trump, as the media tries to make it sound." He said Europe needs strong economic relations with Russia and China, and Trump is pushing in that direction. There is now a great opportunity to create cooperation between Europe and Russia, driven by Trump, and to extend this to Asia.

Zanni concluded by saying Europe needs to have functioning sovereign states, otherwise it will fail.

The interview will be posted by tomorrow. The *Rogue Money* website has a strong following of anti-establishment networks, and its interviews are often reposted by others. It carries a weekly, twenty-minute interview with Schlanger, and is now frequently posting material from LaRouche PAC, with links to the site.